MW01025425

No Place I'd Rather Be

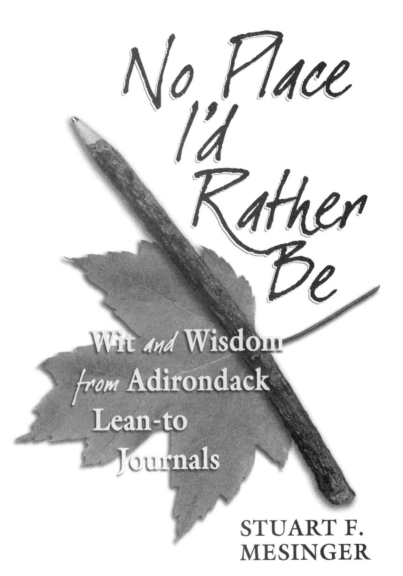

No Place I'd Rather Be

Wit *and* Wisdom *from* Adirondack Lean-to Journals

STUART F. MESINGER

Adirondack
ADK
Mountain Club

Lake George, New York

Copyright © 2006 by Stuart F. Mesinger. All rights reserved.

Cover design by Tamara Dever, © 2006 TLC Graphics, www.TLCGraphics.com
Text design by Ann Hough, ADK
First edition published 2006

Grateful acknowledgment is made to Mark Strand for permission to reprint, on pp. 172–3, "Keeping Things Whole" from *Selected Poems*. Copyright © 1979, 1980 by Mark Strand.

No part of this publication may be reproduced or transmitted in any form or by any means without express written permission from the publisher. Requests for permission should be addressed in writing to the Publications Director of the Adirondack Mountain Club.

Published by the Adirondack Mountain Club, Inc
814 Goggins Road, Lake George, NY 12845-4117
www.adk.org

The Adirondack Mountain Club (ADK) is dedicated to the protection and responsible recreational use of the New York State Forest Preserve, and other parks, wild lands, and waters vital to our members and chapters. The Club, founded in 1922, is a member-directed organization committed to public service and stewardship. ADK employs a balanced approach to outdoor recreation, advocacy, environmental education, and natural resource conservation.

ADK encourages the involvement of all people in its mission and activities; its goal is to be a community that is comfortable, inviting, and accessible.

Library of Congress Cataloging-in-Publication Data

Mesinger, Stuart F., 1958–
  No place I'd rather be: wit and wisdom from Adirondack lean-to journals / Stuart F. Mesinger—1st ed.
    p. cm.
 ISBN-13: 978-1-931951-14-2 (pbk.)
 ISBN-10: 1-931951-14-4 (pbk.)
 1. Hiking—New York (State)—Adirondack Mountains—Anecdotes. 2. Trails—New York (State)—Adirondack Mountains—Anecdotes. 3. Adirondack Mountains—Anecdotes. I. Title.

 GV199.42.N652A34546 2006
 917.47′53—dc22

                    2006005856

Printed in Canada
18 17 16 15 14 13 12 11 10 09 08 07 06   1 2 3 4 5 6 7 8 9 10

Proceed at your own risk.

The often heated opinions expressed in this book's excerpts are those of unknown writers who left their words of wisdom—and lots of other words besides—in the journals ("registers") kept in lean-tos throughout the Adirondacks. We extend our thanks to these individuals, and the illustrators among them, without whom this book would not have been possible or half as much fun. Their opinions, and the tone in which they are delivered, do not reflect the beliefs of the Adirondack Mountain Club or its members and do not have ADK's endorsement.

This book is dedicated to my father, John Mesinger,

who first took me into the woods and taught me

to love the outdoors.

Contents

Preface

IF YOU GO HIKING in the Adirondacks, it won't be long before you come across a lean-to placed in some scenic spot to provide shelter for the passing hiker. If you take a look inside, you're likely to find a journal—known locally as a "register"—stored in a plastic baggie. If you take it out and start to read, you probably won't be going anywhere for a while.

This is a book made up of the interesting things people write in lean-to registers. The entries are by turns inspirational, hilarious, pathetic, and downright crazy, to name just a few moods. They provide insight into the minds and motives of people who, for diverse reasons, have chosen through physical hardship to reach places of solitude, beauty, and sometimes misery and danger.

On the most basic level, the registers are diaries of use and conditions: who was there, what they saw, and what they thought about it. We are reminded every few pages that, more often than not, fireplace smoke blows into the lean-to and mice are brazen thieves. There's lots of rainy weather and countless bugs. Blisters are a frequent topic. We are presented with an excessive number of dinner menus.

More interesting is the writing left behind by persons who have been moved in some way. Their entries often reflect upon their reasons for entering the woods. The regenerative power of nature is a common theme, and so is the Zen of being in the natural world.

Those on spiritual or religious quests, lovers, the anguished, the occasional fool, or worse—all leave a piece of themselves in the registers. There's a lot of fodder for the armchair psychologist, and one can't help playing "name that dysfunction." The fact that the entries were not written for publication, or even for much of an audience, seems to result in a particular honesty that is extremely compelling. Most writers' defenses are down; with the exception of peak-bagging dullards, there is little posturing or bragging.

Best of all are the many souls who give voice to their love of wild places, of solitude, and of the unique experience of carrying your home on your back into a world that is larger and infinitely more alive and complex than the one we normally inhabit.

In the natural world we play only a small part, our impact limited to what we can touch in our daily actions. We feed some bugs and squash others. We dislodge a rock and alter the universe beneath our feet. But in the Big Picture, our control of what goes on is ridiculously limited, at least compared to what we are accustomed to thinking it is. If we allow ourselves to slow down and become aware of what is going on around us, our separation from the natural world diminishes, and as it does, we think more keenly and clearly. I think that's why truth and insight seem to find so many people in the woods.

It isn't all about beauty and nature. There's a lot of playful good humor, as well as crude remarks, and some things that are downright offensive. In this way, the registers are an excellent reflection of the world.

Particularly entertaining is the interplay among the authors. My first exposure to registers was on the Appalachian Trail where through hikers use them to communicate as they play leapfrog on that long trail. Adirondack registers don't display the quirky mind-set of the long-distance hiker, but they do contain a fair amount of debate on just about every imaginable issue.

The inspiration for this book came on a backpacking trip in the West Canada Lakes Wilderness. I was reading the register in one of the West Lake lean-tos when the idea struck that someone ought to make a book out of these entries—and that someone ought to be me. It turns out that the Adirondack Mountain Club, which sponsors an adopter program by which the majority of the lean-tos are maintained and cared for, keeps an archive of old registers. Additionally, several individuals were gracious enough to lend me registers in their care. And so a book was born.

The material in this book is presented largely as it was found in the registers. I've made some minor edits to improve punctuation or, where desperately needed, clarify meaning. For the most part though, you are reading the unretouched thoughts of those who took the time to record them in the registers. Don't blame me for the atrocious grammar you are about to read.

The registers reveal many backwoods archetypes: the campfire story; the bear adventure; the fishing trip; the bug debacle. I've tried to assemble some examples of each with the hope of giving the reader a little of the flavor of an Adirondack hiking trip. By so doing I hope that you, too, may be inspired to enjoy some time in the woods, and like many of the authors on the following pages, come out better for it.

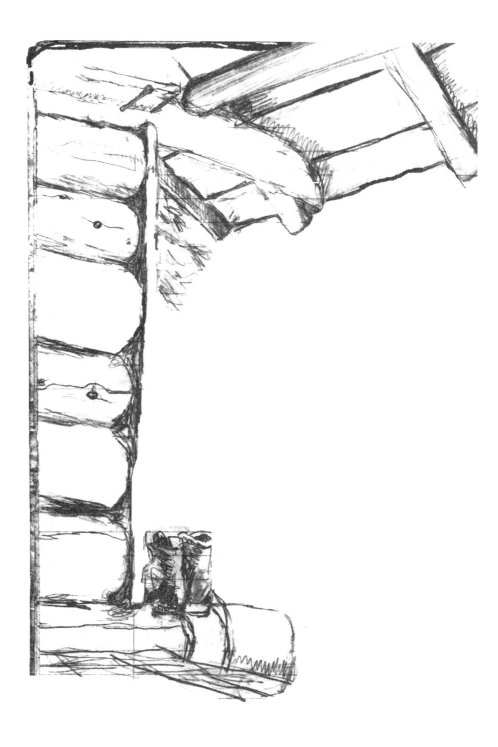

1

Lean-tos

Decided to sleep in lean-to, floors like C-ment. To those who come behind us, bring a mattress.
—GRIFFIN RAPIDS

BEFORE WE EMBARK on our literary journey through the registers, a few paragraphs about the lean-tos themselves.

The first lean-tos were temporary affairs constructed by Adirondack guides to shelter their "sports" from the all-too-frequent rain. The pattern presently in use is believed to be based on a lean-to constructed in the 1890s by the Lyon family on Deer Island in Upper Saranac Lake. In 1919 the Conservation Department began to build lean-tos according to regular plans, with variations in construction style and materials as conditions required. At one time there were more than two hundred fifty in the Adirondacks; the current count is a little over two hundred.

The Conservation Department and its successor, the Department of Environmental Conservation (DEC), attempted to maintain the lean-tos, but their numbers, remoteness, and chronic shortages of ranger time (not to mention more pressing responsibilities) made this a hit-or-miss affair at best. Over time many lean-tos deteriorated, with leaking roofs, rotting floors, and garbage-strewn sites becoming common. The condition of the privies is best left

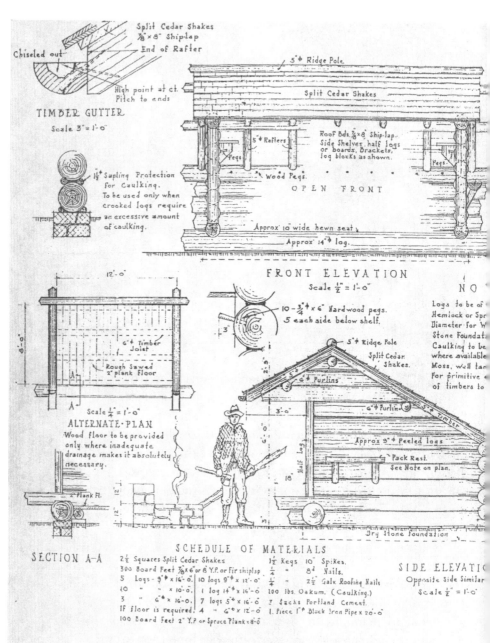

Split Cedar Shakes
⅞"×8" Ship-lap
End of Rafter
Chiseled out

High point at ct.
Pitch to ends

TIMBER GUTTER
Scale 3" = 1'-0"

1½"⌀ Sapling Protection
for Caulking.
To be used only when
crooked logs require
an excessive amount
of caulking.

5"⌀ Ridge Pole

Split Cedar Shakes

Roof Bds. ⅞"×8" Ship-lap.
5"⌀ Rafters
Side Shelves, half logs
or boards, Brackets,
log blocks as shown.

Pegs

Wood Pegs.

OPEN FRONT

Approx 10" wide hewn seat
Approx 14"⌀ log.

FRONT ELEVATION
Scale ½" = 1'-0"

12'-0"

6"⌀ Timber
Joist

Rough Sawed
2" plank Floor

A

Scale ¼" = 1'-0"
ALTERNATE·PLAN
Wood floor to be provided
only where inadequate
drainage makes it absolutely
necessary.

2" Plank Fl.

10 - ¾"⌀ × 6" Hardwood pegs.
5 each side below shelf.

5"⌀ Ridge Pole
Split Cedar
Shakes.

6"⌀ Purlins

6"⌀ Purlin

3'-0"

Approx 9"⌀ Peeled logs
Pack Rest.
See Note on plan.

18"

Dry Stone Foundation

N O

Logs to be of
Hemlock or Spr
Diameter for W
Stone Foundati
Caulking to be
where available
Moss, well tan
For primitive
of timbers to

SECTION A-A

SCHEDULE OF MATERIALS
2¼ Squares Split Cedar Shakes
300 Board Feet ⅞"×6" or 8 Y.P. or Fir shiplap
5 Logs - 9"⌀ × 16'- 0".
10 "   × 10'- 0".
3 "   6"⌀ × 16'- 0.
IF floor is required. 4 " 6"⌀ × 12'- 0"
100 Board Feet 2" Y.P or Spruce Plank×8'-0

1½ Kegs 10" Spikes.
¼ " 8ᵈ Nails.
¼ " 2½" Galv. Roofing Nails
100 lbs. Oakum. (Caulking.)
3 Sacks Portland Cement.
1. Piece 1"⌀ Black Iron Pipe × 20'- 0"
10 logs 9"⌀ × 12'- 0"
1 log 14"⌀ × 16'- 0
7 logs 5"⌀ × 16'- 0

SIDE ELEVATIO
Opposite Side Similar
Scale ½" = 1'-0"

NEW YORK STATE CONSERVATION DEPARTMENT
STANDARD OPEN CAMP OR ADIRONDACK LEAN-TO
Scale ½" = 1'-0" and as shown.

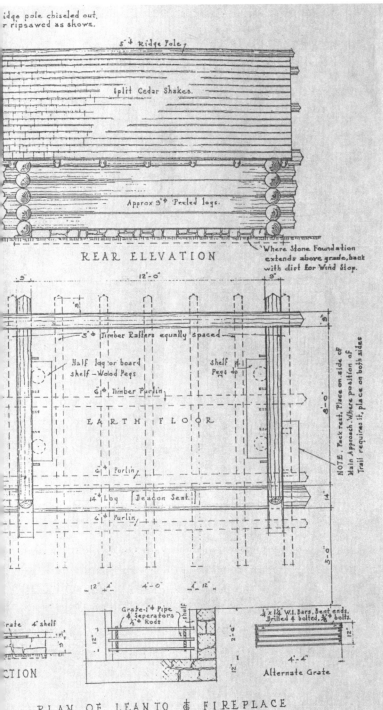

idge pole. chiseled out.
r ripsawed as shown.

5"⌀ Ridge Pole

Split Cedar Shakes.

Approx 9"⌀ Peeled logs.

REAR ELEVATION

Where Stone Foundation
extends above grade, back
with dirt for Wind Stop.

12'-0"

5"⌀ Timber Rafters equally spaced

Half log or board
shelf – Wood Pegs

Shelf
Pegs do

6"⌀ Timber Purlin

EARTH FLOOR

NOTE. Pack rest. Place on side of
Main Approach. Where position of
Trail requires it, place on both sides

6"⌀ Purlin

14"Log [Deacon Seat]

6"⌀ Purlin

12" 4" 4'-0" 4" 12"

Grate-1"⌀ Pipe
4 Seperators
½"⌀ Rods

½ x 1½ W.I. Bars. Bent ends.
Drilled & bolted. ⅜"⌀ bolts.

rate 4" shelf

TION

Alternate Grate

4'-4"

PLAN OF LEAN TO & FIREPLACE

Scale ½" = 1'-0"

FILED WITH C.C.C. AS PLAN NO. 2
J.M.B MAY-1936.

Construction
drawings
published
by the New
York State
Conservation
Department in
the 1930s for
a standard
lean-to, based
on a Civilian
Conservation
Corps design

COURTESY
ADIRONDACK
MUSEUM, BLUE
MOUNTAIN LAKE,
NEW YORK

to the imagination. Volunteers sometimes took it upon themselves to clean and maintain a particular lean-to, but there was no system or order to these efforts.

To remedy this situation, the Adopt-a-Lean-to program was started in 1984 by the Adirondack Mountain Club (ADK) in cooperation with DEC. Eight lean-tos were initially included. The program was an immediate success; within four years 90 had been adopted. In recent years, around 150 of the 212 or so Adirondack lean-tos are adopted each year. Adopters, all of whom are volunteers, visit at least once a year, perform clean-up and general maintenance, and report conditions to the owner, New York State.

Among the duties of the lean-to adopter is the provision and maintenance of the register. These are grammar school composition books, the sturdy lined pages of which assist those with questionable handwriting (approximately 75 percent of the population, from strained observation). The adopters place the register in a Ziploc bag to repel moisture and mice. The hiker finds it on a shelf nailed high on the lean-to wall, where it provides an introduction similar to the hotel services channel at the Ramada.

Small semicircles are often missing from the books, thanks to the insatiable gnawing of resident rodents. Some of the registers retain the fragrance of wood smoke, while those that have been left in the rain are swollen and smell of mildew and damp. Pages are often missing, having been used as fire starter or bum wad. The writing tool alternates from lead to ink and back again, depending on who forgot to return the implement and what the next person carried. Charcoal sticks are still used in these modern times.

WHAT'S IN A NAME?
AND WHO IS LILLIAN BROOK?

This book has adopted the convention of following each excerpt with the name of the lean-to register from which it was quoted. Rather than repeat the word *lean-to* each time, the quote is followed by the place name, set in a different font style.

This can make for some confusion if you are skimming these pages unaware, for example, that Lillian Brook is a place, rather than a person.

Numbered entries can also be misleading. Bushnell Falls has several lean-tos in the vicinity, hence Bushnell Falls 1 and Bushnell Falls 2—and Cold River 3, Duck Hole 2, and so forth.

The region's peculiar history has also wormed its way into the matter of naming. Two lean-tos located on the site of the former Santa Clara Lumber Company Camp Number Four bear part of that name—to odd effect. Thus *Number Four 1* and *Number Four 2* appear in these pages as well.

The official purpose of the registers is public safety. A hiker who has recorded his or her presence has left a clue if a search ever becomes necessary. Registers are one of the first things consulted by rangers searching for a missing hiker.

The registers usually begin with a cheerful introductory note from the adopters and some brief instructions, often specific to the location. For example:

WIT, WISDOM—AND SOME VERY POOR CHOICES

The observant reader will note several admonitions to bad behavior in this preamble, and I'm afraid there are many examples recorded in the registers. People do all kinds of stupid things in the woods (OK, people do all kinds of stupid things everywhere). Sometimes they write about them, with glee even.

If you keep reading, you're going to find some examples. They have been included because, in addition to beautiful sunsets, moments of enlightenment, and sore feet, they too represent a part of the experience of being in the woods, and because they are instructive in a "don't-do-this" sort of way.

One of ADK's major functions is to educate the public about appropriate backcountry practices. Thus, publishing some of what you are about to read required a little fortitude on the part of the author and ADK.

It's worth taking a moment to review some of the major principles of responsible backcountry behavior, in particular Leave No Trace principles (Appendix 1) and Forest Preserve Regulations (Appendix 2), and to keep them in mind as you read this book. The reader is invited to visit www.adk.org and www.dec.state.ny.us to learn more about responsible backcountry practices.

Hello! Please don't burn this book … We've adopted Cedar Point lean-to, and we ask that you sign in and write down any comments you wish. We have several suggestions.

Hang all your food. Even if for 5 minutes, the bears around here are amazingly skillful at separating you from your dinner. Last year, one particular bear (Jim) scored a perfect 16 bags of food from 16 consecutive campers.

Filter or boil all water. Consider all sources contaminated.

Please use only dead and down wood for small fires—if this area is badly denuded DEC will remove this lean-to.

Please, please pack out your trash, and if you can, maybe a little extra. If you have a fire, you could scout the area for burnables left by less considerate hikers. Check fire pit for aluminum & tin & pack it out.

We turn in this register next year to the DEC, and they use it to help determine how this area will be utilized. YOUR COMMENTS ARE HELPFUL AND APPRECIATED. Please leave the broom for the next group.

THANKS TO EVERYONE FOR KEEPING CEDAR POINT SO NICE AND CLEAN.
—CEDAR POINT

HEADS LIST OF UNNEEDED CRAP

TOO MANY CLOTHES
ASS POWDER
FIRST AID KIT
SPARE BOOTS (15 lbs)
KITCHEN SINK
6 PACK (MAYBE NOT)

COULD OF TREATED EVERYONE AT WOODSTOCK

Robs
PLAYSKOOL
BACKPACK

(BABY COULD EASILY CARRY IT TO SUMMIT)

BRAND PROM

TEAM
Berpacks

WISH LIST
SHERPA...

WAIT
5 SHERPAS
& A
DONKEY!!!

- IN THE DISTANCE

2

Registers

Gary, I would like a copy of the Ouluska Pass log book. I am ten years old and like reading the logs. I did not get to finish that one so can you please send me one. Thank you very much. P.S. I am ten.
—COLD RIVER 3

T HE REGISTERS ARE A DIARY of place and time. They are the hiker's essential firsthand record, noting the condition of the water supply at the spring, the level of mouse activity, and the number of grub-stealing bruins in the vicinity. They are also trip records. They tell of friendships and weather, meals and campfires, destinations and adventures. They also serve as sounding boards and confessionals. They are full of musings on religion, philosophy, and politics, as well as deeply personal reflections. They contain debates on nearly every topic imaginable, including the contents of the registers themselves.

We hiked Saddleback and Basin ended up here. I would like to point out the serious state of our education. For example, these past few pages are filled with grammatical errors and syntax mistakes. Hey even dolphins are capable of interpreting sentence structure. If you ask me maybe some of those people should spend more time in the classroom and less out here in the wilderness.
—BUSHNELL FALLS 1

Unfortunately, I'm not much of a photographer, so this book can't always convey the context of the registers. It's much easier to appreciate "the beautiful scene in front of me" when you are staring at it (which makes the comment unnecessary in a way, but let's not quibble). Even when filled with writing that wouldn't pass a sixth grade composition exam (*The forest has never seen such sin and abuse of the English language. I hope the forest forgives us and welcomes us in the future … Rocky Falls*), there is a unique feeling of connection in sitting in the place where others sat before you, looking at what they saw, and musing on the juxtaposition of time, place, and thought that results. Some lean-to adopters type up the contents of their old registers and leave them in the lean-to. But Heisenberg's Uncertainty Principle tells us that the act of perceiving something changes that which is perceived.

Mountain brooks sing of unpredictability
Their dips and falls and turns
Wherever the contours take them.

—LILLIAN BROOK

Does it do something to the literary process of "register signing" when the writer knows that the words are to be typed, and, no doubt, Xeroxed, even? It makes the process more abstract, removed from life by one more step beyond the intimacy of struggling to discern the initials you carved 15 or 20 years ago. Perhaps I'm thinking like that because at Plumleys 2 nights ago I used part of the old lean-to left as firewood and saw old initials go into the fire. Felt weird; perhaps its good to save the words on secure vellum, but a lot of the poetry of the messy boy carving and scratching is knowing that it fades, rots, maybe burns.
—OULUSKA PASS

The registers are a unique means of communication, related to the wall in the public restroom in that one's musings are posted for all to see, but allowing for much broader content. In a way, they are the forerunner of the Internet.

This register and those in other adopted lean-tos may be the most interesting literary form being practiced these days on this side of Champlain, and the lean-to adoption program one of the most successful ADK–DEC/cooperative efforts I know of. From reading the entries you get a feeling for just how successful it is. Every visit, every entry, adds another dimension to the true commentary of this place. Imagine what the entries will be like when the moose and the wolf are back here at full-strength.
—BOQUET RIVER

Construction of lean-tos helped open the backcountry to wider use by providing shelter from the harsh and unpredictable weather of the Adirondacks. This opening of the "inn" to public use led in turn to a variety of questions of etiquette, the most basic of which is whether the first to arrive is required to share the lean-to with subsequent travelers. (Oddly, the regulation requiring that lean-tos be shared is not posted on the wall.) This question takes on added importance in inclement weather. Absent direction, two schools of thought have formed, summarized as follows.

Assholes came and acted like site was theirs. Ate lunch and threw food around, moved my stuff and hung out. Two named Sam and Adrian. I don't know about law but courtesy says ask to stop at taken site. The whole damn forest and they can't move 100 yards away to eat lunch. If I wanted company I'd visit relatives, not come here.
—WOLF POND

And:

Maybe I'm just whining but we arrived at Ward Brook Lean-to in the midst of a downpour to find two individuals sprawled out using every inch of the lean-to. In my experi-

ence, hiking etiquette requires them to make room for us even though these two lean-tos are only 10–15 minutes away. It was after all a downpour and it continued to rain for a half hour. They could have at least offered a place to sit until the rain stopped. No not a word: Just the feeling you get when someone knows they have to do something but wishes whatever it is would go away. In conversation between themselves one had the gall to talk about how tough it is to dry out. If they even offered an explanation why we couldn't stay [it would have helped] *but there was none forthcoming. I've never run into this before. Hikers are a courteous lot. I'm blowing off steam but also asking those few who are unaware of what they are doing or just plain selfish to get with the program.*
—NUMBER FOUR 2

Fortunately, the prevailing opinion goes like this.

I've come to the conclusion, after years of camping in these parts, for the solitary or private camping experience—pitch a tent, don't expect one if you are in a lean-to. These are for all who can fit. It's not first come first serve. We've stayed with some others and some others have stayed with us. It is part of the lean-to "experience" and has always been memorable.
—LILLIAN BROOK

Lean-to adopters provide basic housekeeping services on their visits and sometimes organize work parties for minor repairs. Major repairs are usually handled by the landlord in Albany. *Lean-to is in nice shape but it needs a floor. Ask DEC to buy you one. Lillian Brook.* The lean-tos are sometimes treated with preservative to prolong their life, and adopters often leave a rake or broom to sweep the floor. Not all approve.

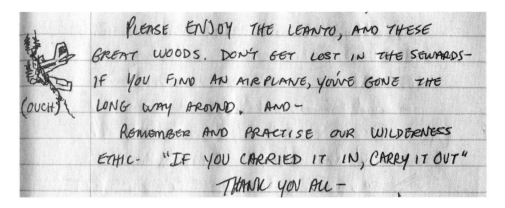

PLEASE ENJOY THE LEANTO, AND THESE
GREAT WOODS. DON'T GET LOST IN THE SEWARDS—
IF YOU FIND AN AIRPLANE, YOU'VE GONE THE
LONG WAY AROUND. AND—
REMEMBER AND PRACTISE OUR WILDERNESS
ETHIC- "IF YOU CARRIED IT IN, CARRY IT OUT"
THANK YOU ALL—

(OUCH)

Lean-to's in great shape, new floor and recently stained and pretty clean. But hey—you forgot to take out the leftover stain with ya! Is this ADK or DEC or HIJKLMNOP? I noted the same conditions today at Big Shallow and Little Shallow Lean-tos. Yesterday, on the path to the Plains from High Falls Trail, I noted leftover metal edge, 3-gallon plastic jugs of stain, and other maintenance debris, just dumped along the way. It's a shame that maintenance crews are exempt from "Pack it in, Pack it out" and some other rules of forest etiquette.

I really don't understand the new rakes, brooms and shovels at the lean-tos. That's a pretty serious investment for visitors to the wilderness. Kinda' makes the wilderness seem a lot more like home. Trouble is, it's not supposed to! Let's keep the Wilderness Forever Wild and get rid of all this hardware, it doesn't belong here.
—WOLF LAKE

In fact, the registers occasionally contain an entry expressing the view that lean-tos don't belong in the wilderness at all, but this is hardly the prevailing opinion. Others express concerns of a different kind.

You might consider telling the lean-to it's adopted. Future trauma could be avoided if the lean-to doesn't already

know. Being none of my business, in a sense, I didn't dare say anything.
—WANIKA FALLS

The following sort of entry is found in the register of every lean-to that has sheltered a hiker from the rain—which is to say, all of them.

Where would we hikers be without these Adirondack lean-tos? Last night it rained ferociously and I would not have been a very happy gaucho if I did not have this shelter over my head. I came in from Cold River lean-to #3 (Shattuck Clearing) after three days of weather along Long Lake so perfect that I lazed along there instead of getting my body in here where it is really beautiful. I was almost tempted to stay at the Seward lean-to since it was beginning to rain but the rather dilapidated looks of that structure gave me second thoughts (they should rename it the Sewer lean-to; shouldn't some work be done on that one, good Ranger Gary?). I got into this wonderful lean-to just when it started pouring and boy did it come down. There was lightning and very high winds all night as well.

But yesterday in the afternoon and early evening it was all very beautiful to watch from the shelter of this fine lean-to. I thought it fortunate that my human eyes, as a brief visitor, were given the gift of sharing in the beauty that goes on here every day. It clears a man's thoughts and wakes him up concerning the things in life which are really important: not money, success, stocks and bonds, but the relationships with people, inner peace, understanding (and for me love and faith in God) which make everything else meaningful. I am thankful for these lean-tos for making the sojourns of all the good people who use these trails so much better (and drier). May we always have them.
—OULUSKA PASS

Despite the less than occasional disagreements, most visitors seem to concur that the contents of the registers have a place in the stilling of the conscious that seems to occur in the woods, a theme to which the entries return more than once.

Reading this register brings back so many good memories (just proves the stimuli of an onrushing brook—the creative juices flow, and the wit runs rampant …) Haven't been here since April 1976, but the "song remains the same", albeit much cleaner. Thank you caretakers for your concentrated effort … After reading all your thoughts and introspective addendos, I agree—the Adirondacks is the place for such meanderings—regardless of politics.
—WANIKA FALLS

3

Take My Advice

Some one should suggest a book of excerpts culled from these registers over the years, if you haven't thought of it already.
—Fɪsʜ Pᴏɴᴅ 1

PRETTY MUCH EVERY ONE of my camping buddies considers himself a master woodsman. It seems there are a lot of camping experts out there who aren't shy about sharing their experience. Because hiking and camping are activities often pursued alone, or with a few friends who have heard it all before, the registers often provide a podium from which didacts can enlighten their fellow travelers.

Nice lean-to, but a few suggestions:

1. Teach birds to eat bugs!
2. More water a little closer to lean-to and make bigger pools for bathing!
3. Although we have not had rain (knock on wood!) canopy should be built over picnic table!
4. Rig several blocks & tackles for permanent bear bag placements!
5a. Arrange for delivery of the NY Times to the privy!
5b. Install 60-watt lighting fixture in privy for late night & early morning research!
5c. Stock inventory of bathroom tissue!
6. There should be a tablecloth and service for 8!

7. Build covered woodshed and stock some!
8. Bicycle should be available for use at Blueberry!
9. Broom (serious!)
10. Microwave would be nice! And a Jenn-Air!
11. Install cold table & stock kegs of Matts and Molson at rear of lean-to!
12. Refinish floors!
13. Decorative wall hangings!
—WARD BROOK

Some don't so much offer advice as make helpful suggestions.

We saw wood shaped like different animals and different kinds of mushrooms and had a good time. The walk was a wonderful experience for the younger children! You do need to remove the broken tree about 1/4 mile down the trail.
—BERRYMILL POND.

The author above may not have been aware that there are in fact those engaged in this very activity.

I have a few suggestions. The trail is very muddy. It needs bog bridges. Someone should come in with a chainsaw and build some. Oh, wait, we are the ADK trail crew! We can do it ourselves. But chainsaws are illegal now, so we will use razor-sharp double bit axes, a crosscut, and 10,000 calories a day for fuel. Enjoy our new bridges just south of the turnoff.
—WANIKA FALLS

Some just complain.

Why did you take out all the nails? Nails are good for:
Hanging flashlights
Spoons, forks

Packs
Bags
Guns
Knifes
Cups
Compass
Lanterns

The roof leaks! Shingles.
Take the garbage from behind the lean-to.
—*WALLFACE*

But more often the tongue is firmly in cheek.

Plumbing needs fixing, toilet does not stop running. Board on outhouse needs fixing. Lean-to could use caulking. Rocks need velcro. Fireplace needs a flu. Trees need trimming on other side of lake.
—*O'NEIL FLOW*

Could you also adopt the outhouse? It needs a coat hook and door. The plumbing did not work and the pizza we ordered arrived cold. Thank you for the dry lean-to.
—*WANIKA FALLS*

However, there's a reason for the title of this book, and it's because the typical entry goes something like this.

In terms of suggestions just some mild improvements here and there. If you people take some of these suggestions too seriously in ten years I could come back to find a paved road in to a state campsite. Things are fine the way they are now. Try not to lose any sleep over some finding bumps in the lean-to floor. Happy with things the way they are.
—*WANIKA FALLS*

4

My First Camping Trip

Had a great time on my first hiking trip (on daddy's back).
—CASCADE POND

EVERYBODY REMEMBERS his or her first camping trip. Mine occurred with the Boy Scouts. After a few weeks as a Tenderfoot, I was looking forward to the jamboree to be held in the far-off woods, a three-mile hike over a steep mountain. My enthusiasm quickly waned as my fellow eleven-year-olds and I took turns lugging our scoutmaster's beer cooler over the switchbacks on a steamy July day.

I retired from scouting shortly thereafter to discover the joys of solo camping. My first experience, at age fifteen, was memorable. I planned a ten-mile loop in the Shenandoah National Park, with walking times and favorable resting places carefully noted on the map. I planned to spend the night in a shelter (the Shenandoah version of the Adirondack lean-to; think stone foundation and more mice), where I would have reliable water and a roof in case it rained.

My mother dropped me off with tearful pleas to take care of myself before she returned to the trailhead the next day. The morning was eventful: I met a copperhead and a rattlesnake, and expanded my sexual education considerably

In the great hall
Of a high mountain
Lake in the court of
The northern windgusts
Announced by ancient pines
An audience with the
Mallow rose on shore
Who nods polite
Acknowledgement
To each in
Turn.

—STEPHENS POND

when I encountered two women entwined in a sunny glade. I enjoyed an early dinner in the shelter, and as I was digesting it encountered a genuine woods hippy who invited me back to his camp. It lay about a half mile from the main trail near the shelter, up a small stream, not at all noticeable.

He had built a sort of tree house accessed by a vine ladder, in which he slept and communed with the forest. A couple of six packs lay cooling in the stream, and there were more than a few baggies of pot scattered about the camp. After a brief tour, my host began smoking an ornately carved pipe and offered to introduce me to the wonders of marijuana, which he assured me would greatly increase my appreciation of the surrounding woodland scene.

After a few hits, I began to feel both strange and distinctly ill at ease. I left as politely as was possible given a total departure time of about ten seconds, and fled down the stream to the trail, convinced that I was about to be murdered by a dope-crazed fiend. As dusk was approaching—well, it seemed that way; actually it was about three hours off, but I hadn't done this sort of thing before—I searched frantically for a hiding place. (The shelter was out of the question; that was the first place he would look.) I finally decided to lose myself in the deep woods and crashed a few hundred yards into the brush, where I crouched, sweating, listening for footsteps.

When the coast seemed clear I decided to construct a temporary shelter, a primitive lean-to, from brush and limbs. (Although my time in the scouts had been short, I had studied well.) I accomplished this with a fair amount of skin lost to the brambles, but I was pleased to be camouflaged and hidden from danger. I lay down, but sleep eluded me. In fact, it escaped me entirely.

The night was not without interest, however. A pair of chipmunks spent the dark hours running across my chest transporting, in cheekful loads, the roll of toilet paper I had placed by my head in case of the sniffles. After several hours of debate (or maybe it was five minutes), I convinced myself that packing the tissue away was far too risky; the rodents might well be rabid and I didn't want to risk them biting me out of anger at losing their supply of fresh bedding. So I spent the night as a speed bump on the Charmin highway. I also discovered that rocks and sticks grow in proportion to the time spent lying on them and that it would have been a good idea to fill a water bottle before retiring.

I was up and on the trail somewhere on the early side of first light, and reached my pick-up point by 8 AM, or about six hours early. When my mother arrived I informed her (as well as my incredulous little brother) that I had had a marvelous time and couldn't wait to do it again. Which was completely true.

First trips, whether alone or with family and friends, are almost always memorable, as these accounts illustrate.

This is my first trip to the mountains and I am here being forced to write in this log by my fiancé. He has been in the area several times and is enjoying himself immensely. We came here from Lake Durant Campground just for a day hike and the trail had a lot of trees down and was bug ridden. It was fun but home is beginning to beckon.

P.S. This is Jay. It is so hard to get these city gals out of the city and into the woods. I think she did enjoy herself. I hope so. I want to come back next year.
—STEPHENS POND

Well, well, well where to start? The frozen toes and fingers and children who can't stop picking up snow or stepping in puddles, the wife who decides to hike little Marcy at 3:00 without telling anyone, or taking a flashlight or food or 1st aid kit who by 1 hour past dark was nowhere to be found. While Tim and John try to figure out which trail to find her, who should stay with the children, besides getting completely worried. We got two other campers down and across the brook worried as well, they were suited up & ready to form a search party when we hear Jacquelyn a coming round the mountain. Finally had dinner. Restless sleeps although everyone said they heard me snoring quite often.

Morning came nice toasty fire, enough to melt Tim's boots. And then there's the 11 year old that tells no one he's never done a #2 in the woods and comes back complaining that he fell in someone else's "pile." From his ankles to his hips melted chocolate chip and I got to wipe him dry. Aghhhhhh! Gonna' come back real soon all alone.
—BUSHNELL FALLS 1

Party of six—This was Shane's first trip to the Adirondacks, he's 7. Arrived here on Saturday. Girls stayed at Camp. Seth bathing while guys hiked to Center Pond. Got attacked by mosquitoes. Girls got sunburned. Had some heavy passing rainstorms in early evening. Sunday after breakfast took hike all the way to Irishtown. Long hike for all of us. Shane did especially well. Lunch at Irishtown and hike back. Sunday evening we raced psychedelic sap rockets in the pond by gathering sap and dipping the ends of twigs in the fir sap and settling them in the pond. Had rain again Sunday evening. Saw leeches, squirrel, loons, and heard a mouse and a coyote.

P.S. And good ghost stories.
—STONY POND

9/5/87 - Nice Hike in, Nice Accommodations, Nice Dog on Roof. Grant was crowded with fast-talking foreigners. Partly cloudy. Nice.

Me, Hubby and Dog out for a hike to get away from it all— were here in the 70's with our 3 kids and no experience in backpacking. Got a lean-to though! Left our 3 kids with total strangers to go back for our supplies—can you imagine doing that in the 90's ??! It has made me thankful I had my kids young—I'm a grandma now and hopefully will bring my grandson here someday—It's great to be here if only for a day.
—PHARAOH LAKE 1

Well we finally made it to the lean-to. Was a tiresome but exciting trip, as I brought my 5 year old son on his first hike. We loved it. There are the 3 of us, myself (Keith) my

son (Joshua) and our very good buddy (Craig). We collected some wood for the fire and are going to spend the night in the lean-to, to heck with the tents. I expected my son to complain the whole way up here but it was him who kept myself and Craig going. Every time we stopped for a rest he kept saying, "Come on guys, let's go." What a special little man he is. He toasted marshmallows or as he calls them smashmellows and enjoyed them. The best thing is he carried his own backpack up the mountain. All the credit to him for that feat. I guess this is the time for him to learn how to hike. Father and son time. Quality time well spent. Hopefully the Adirondacks will always be here for all generations. Happy hiking.
—MR. VAN

We hoped to go to Wanika Falls along the North-ville–Placid Trail from Lake Placid but my 11 year old daughter couldn't carry her backpack so we came back to our old friend the Henderson Lean-To, so I could carry in my backpack & then go back and get hers. That worked fine except we lost her stuffed animal along the way.
— WALLFACE

Only one suggestion—if you want to enjoy the beauty of this pond properly do leave your 3-yr-old with a babysitter!
—STEPHENS POND

5

Love Stories

It was a glorious day here—in the 50's and about 5" of virgin snow. My boyfriend Joe and I cut a path for Summit Rock. Overlooking the lake, surrounded by mountains and with the sun shining down, he asked me to marry him. I said yes! Happy trails and happier holidays!! The future Liz S.
—WALLFACE

EVERYBODY READS "THE PERSONALS" once in a while. At least, I think they do. I've only known one person to answer an ad though. She was a sporty number, unable to find a guy who shared her love of the outdoors in general and hiking in particular. The ad she answered looked promising enough. "SM, tall, professional, attractive, athletic seeks SF to share weekend camping, hiking and canoe adventures in the Adirondacks." The contact was made and they agreed to scope each other out over dinner at a trendy Mexican place. Unfortunately, and the worst of all possibilities (including basic hygiene problems as far as I'm concerned), he proved to be a gearhead who spent the next three hours regaling her with a detailed history of the lightweight stove cleaning attachments he had owned and loved. She couldn't have done any worse had she answered a personal in the registers.

I am a single, tall, lanky fellow looking for a good looking 5 ft 3 in or taller, hair not a preference, 90–138 lbs. SWF,

who likes camping, 4x4ing and one who can enjoy comfortable silences. Leave picture of 4x4.
—GRIFFIN RAPIDS

During the summer of 1993, the Trout Pond register served as a virtual bulletin board for boys and girls looking to get together.

Spent night at [campsite] #44, took boat to here, not staying in lean to but maybe 100 ft. from it. Here with Jamie and Ron, leaving tomorrow at 5. Don't want to go back to the old grind. Lean-to in great condition, met a lot of people on the trail. Been coming here since I was a kid, now 21, name's Greg, single, so if there's any available women out there write me.
—TROUT POND

Hey Gregg, We have 2 available women here—area code 516—zip code 11793. Sight #35— look it up in the book [register]. Women are shy—please write us.
—TROUT POND

Hello we're the girls that stayed at Salmon Lake this weekend. Now our canoe is gone—we hope a friend borrowed it, if not we have enough food for 1 day left. Help! … A very nice ranger stopped by to check on us, noticed our canoe was gone. She is giving Nancy a ride to see if "friend" borrowed our canoe. We're rescued either way—Thank God because I hungry for Mickey D's. Bye Now.
—TROUT POND

Sorry to read about your canoe, me and my buddy (not "good buddies") Dave saw a white fiberglass one down the shore a bit, hope you found your "friend." We are camped at #21 (Stillwater Reservoir, I can't spell it!) and we would be happy to treat you to Mickey D's.
—TROUT POND

The preceding entries lead logically to this one, where the written advertisement is replaced by the face-to-face meeting. Most male readers will be able to relate to this tale of stray-dog lust. I will spare the reader my own pitiful yearnings in this vein, other than to note that I once took an afternoon off from a lengthy Appalachian Trail hike to watch a girls' softball team practice. Unlike these characters, I never got up the nerve to say hello.

Matt and I are wrapping up our award winning tour of the Piseco to Blue Mtn. Lake section of the Northville–Placid Trail. Our purely male dreams were answered last night when we rolled into the Cedar River lean-to. Upon our arrival we were greeted by the Cornell University Orientation Group. There were four nice looking lasses clad only in sports bras frolicking in the water. Of course, there were some males in this group, but who cares. It was such a perfect situation; this lean-to was the only one within 5 or so miles, it was getting dark, thunder was rumbling, and we had just walked 13 miles.

Obviously there wasn't any room for us in the lean-to, so we pitched our tent (no pun intended sick-o's) right next to it. We explained our semi-pathetic situation to the leaders. One happened to be a sexy, dark haired, cute, smiling girl about our age (21), and the other was a long-haired hippie type guy. They had no qualms about us hanging out. I know this sounds like one of those letters in Penthouse, but this is true, trust me.

Anyways, we made dinner and then decided to polish off

the Brew-skis we lugged over 30 miles. The leaders of the group got a little nervous about us drinking around the impressionable little toddlers, so they pulled us aside to have a little chat. We convincingly explained how we had found these beers (four) jettisoned in a lean-to far back and that we damned well deserved them after what we had been through. Once again they had no qualms. Since our four beers were gone we jumped right in to an iced tea Jim Beam cocktail out of an elegant Nalgene bottle. I'm not sure if they knew we were hitting the hooch, but at least it wasn't obvious.

About this time we decided to build a fire. The only safe place to make a fire was, of course, in front of the lean-to. Tapping into our alcohol fueled, testosterone injected man power, we went to town hauling in giant trees and then reducing them into perfect sized logs with a hatchet. I think our little caveman exhibition might have stirred some lust in the hearts of those four girls. We were strong men, we came, we gave them fire. If this isn't the most primitive pick-up technique, I don't know what is.

I know you would all like to hear how we swooned the women into our tent and had steamy sex, but nothing like that happened. Instead they played some group building games while we sat around and got drunk. We ended up going to our tent and passing out only to be roused by a ferocious rainstorm. The next morning we had breakfast and said farewell. What the hell happens to men in the wilderness? Does being surrounded by trees tap into some hidden reservoir of horniness?
—CASCADE POND

Fortunately, the registers often report more romantic encounters. For example, what could be more romantic than a mountaintop proposal? The following backwoods wedding announcement was copied and distributed in registers throughout the High Peaks region.

Long challenging hike on the Seward Range; thinking I wouldn't be able to do all three, but low and behold; waiting for me at the top of Seward was the greatest surprise of my life! A MARRIAGE PROPOSAL AND A DIAMOND RING! Hate to inform all you single women but I just became the luckiest woman in the world and will get to wake up to the kindest, sweetest, dearest man on God's green earth. I thought there was nothing more peaceful and joyful to the soul then time in the 'Dacks; but yesterday surpassed all my dreams. I'll never stop coming to this great wilderness and now will have a long-lasting partnership with my hiker-camper-buddy. Thanks Chris. I love you for all of this.
—BLUEBERRY

I wonder if Campmoor has a bridal registry? Couples truly committed to the outdoors have been known to reserve the honeymoon suite at their favorite lean-to: *Spending the weekend here on my honeymoon, the rest is none of your damn business! Rocky Falls.* Others use them for dates.

Crazy as this may sound, I have taken a wonderful woman I met via the internet here on our first weekend "together." Having had her flown in all the way from Irvine, California, we (I) opted to take her here where I had been many times before, wanting to show her the beauty of New York State and what better place than the Adirondacks, being an avid hiker, and her as well. We knew this would be romantic. It has lived up to its billing. My cyber love is now eager to move to this wonderful state and we will no doubt bring our children to where we spent our first "real" time together.
—MUD LAKE

You may detect a theme here, and yes, sex is frequently a topic. The cruder entries are often scribbled over or torn out by self-appointed censors (and now that I have a child of impressionable age, I thank them, sort of), but some nuggets remain. The archetypical entry goes something like this.

Mm, aaa, Hi I'm Bill and my wife oooh, are just visiting well I got to go. (mooore, please stop, ooooh!) Screaming,
—WOLF POND

The couple below recorded their lovemaking in registers throughout the Adirondacks. For them, the woods did indeed have a transformative effect.

Bill and I came here to spend a relaxing weekend. I've always been a strong believer in women's issues and have never been into pain, but Bill suggested that we get into mild spankings. Reluctantly, I agreed. Bill was artful with the pine bough. That night became a whole new adventure in my life. I now understand that my life was destined to become a true master/slave relationship. Thank you for letting me share this with you and for letting me express my thoughts.
—PHARAOH

There are those who like to watch.

Just met a cute couple who hiked in from Long Lake for a swim. (If I meet your parents I'll tell them you weren't doing what they maybe were afraid you were doing).
—COLD RIVER 4

For those supposing the Adirondacks' ravenous insect life is a deterrent, think again.

This is not our first outdoor experience but it is the first time that we are able to have sex without being stopped by rangers or sudden newcomers. Actually, the black flies tried,

but they were not persuasive enough!
—HIGH FALLS EAST

Sometimes the registers record love's blossoming. This entry covered several pages in alternating his-and-hers handwriting.

He said: My day started late in the afternoon but for some reason I had to make it to Klondike Lean to.

She said: My day started, no, my day ended by deciding to take the lean-to instead of camping on the ground because the sky looked threatening—so Karen, Tom & I set up our camp at Klondike camp. We were dreading having anyone come join us because we wanted to be alone.

He said: As darkness approached rapidly—and thunderstorms came over the ridge—He thought he would never find the lean-to. Cussing himself for leaving so late—his thoughts drifted to who might be in the lean-to. Catching a whiff of wood smoke, he walked up to the lean-to and found ...

She said: We wanted to be alone because the previous night we were forced to stay in a lean-to w/Ward & June Cleaver. Anyway here comes this really interesting young man ...

He said: Oh my—one guy and 2 girls—this was much better than having to share the site w/22 guys ...

She said: We ended up talking all night because we couldn't sleep (just the interesting young man Dave & myself)— We drank lots of ginger brandy & watched the moonlight hit the trees & ended up getting comfortable & ... & now I have his address & the story continues.
—KLONDIKE

The following set of entries, some of my very favorite, appeared over a period of years at the Streeter Lake lean-to in St. Lawrence County.

Last night we came in by canoe at 10:00 p.m. Set up and cooked hamburgers. We talked by the fire and moonlight till 12:30 a.m. Then made love until 2:30 a.m. I've never slept outside and never been loved in such a perfect way. Morning came, Steve cooked me eggs while I slept. We went for a walk to Streeter Mt. I'm 28 and a dream just came true. Thanks for a wonderful guy who loves me enough to help my dreams come true.

P.S. Stand by for the wedding. We're getting married here. Priscilla & Steve & baby?
—*Streeter Lake*

Although they didn't get married at Streeter Lake, Steve and Priscilla kept coming back.

Steve and Priscilla here for two nights and days just to spend some time alone. No kids, no cars, no noise, just us! We fell in love here three years ago & have been here every year to keep the spark going. Well instead of a spark this year we had a fire. Must be the magic of Streeter. We canoed and walked to Franes for a little hunting. Didn't see any but that's okay. We didn't really plan on taking anything from this beautiful place except the bag of garbage left by the persons before us. I guess they had more to carry than we had in our two trips. Have to go back to the rat race tomorrow. Good thing we have each other and Streeter!

P.S. We went dipping at Crystal Lake it was cold & calm but very awakening. Don't know how the loons do it. Maybe that's why there so loved!!
—*Streeter Lake*

Honeymoon Poem

John
I hiked up to find water so green
In the north where the air is so clean
One week married to my new queen.
Placid has shopping and stores full of stuff
A little of that and I've had enough
We'd rather be here where the edges are rough.

Susan
I have a new husband
His name is John
We're going swimming
With no clothes on!

I hope no one sees us
'Cause I'll turn all red
But later tonight
Right after we're fed
I'm sure we're going
To be naked in bed!

—COPPERAS POND

They came alone and they came with their family.

   Came up about 8:00. No one was here. Started out not so good. The kids fought & the dog got about 50 porcupine quills. Almost went home but the kids went to bed and the dog, well, was a little less adventurous. So Steve and I watched the fire and Saturday was beautiful and we ate breakfast, went swimming, ate lunch, went swimming, ate supper, went canoeing. Tried to fish but where are they? Saturday night about 15 people came. Sunday we ate breakfast, cleaned up camp, went back to Crystal for a swim and then headed back to the real world. This place always makes us feel a little more in love with each other and nature! Steve and Priscilla.
—STREETER LAKE

Streeter Lake became a touchstone in their lives, a place to which they returned for renewal year after year.

Steve, Priscilla, Ryan and Karrie and Jasmine came to spend the night. Lean-to was full, stayed in the potato field. It rained all night but beautiful today. We are headed for a swim up to Crystal. The kids had fun: no chores to do. As for Romeo & Juliet, we are more in love than the last time. This is a magical, peaceful place and better than any marriage or family counselor.
—STREETER LAKE

Priscilla and Steve in for a canoe ride and peace. Can't stay long but the trees are beautiful, the sky clear and the birds are singing. We're in love as always. Probably the next time we will be camping and hunting, although Steve has already got his little white tail. I think that's why we never get a deer anymore.
—STREETER LAKE

Hunters, anglers, parents, lovers. Steve and Priscilla are regular people who found a connection to each other and an anchor for their lives in a little corner of the woods.

ADVANCE PLANNING

In the morning
I'm gonna' go up on the mountain.
Get some sun.

By noontime I'll be off
In the forest sleep'n where
The moss grows soft.

Come evening—might hike
Down to the honeybee tree

But for the night-time
My sweet-lipped-soft-cheeked
Warm-armed charm'n darlin'
I'm come'n right back home to thee

—COWHORN POND

Tall Tales

Saw Elvis and Bigfoot playing cards down by the old Beaver Dam.
—STEPHENS POND

A RECURRENT REGISTER FEATURE is the tall tale. Several themes appear regularly.

• My party was attacked by a giant bear/beaver/sasquatch. With these … dying words … I warn yo— (style points for extravagantly scrawled final letters).
• The popular death and dismemberment series, of which the most common variant is, "I am a crazed madman, my party is buried behind the lean-to, *you're next!*"
• The fish in this lake are four feet long, and I found some buried gold. Here's a map to find it (page invariably torn).

Nearly every register contains a few whoppers. Even if you've read a dozen variants of the story, they're still fun.

What a great place! Killed my companion yesterday; he ate the last twinkie. He's buried 500 steps to the left, so don't dig for worms there. Please leave the place as nice as you found it.
—OXSHOE POND

Oct. 1, '96. I'm alone now. The last survivor… the chipmunks have taken my entire party. First it was Jeff. He went quietly, no one noticed for hours. Then Susan—a screamer. Scott, Steve and Mike disappeared near the falls. I am scared that they are waiting for me now to leave the lean-to. Wait, I hear something large moving in brush. It's a chipmunk—at least 400 lbs! And a shredded North Fall jacket stuck in its teeth (Jeff's!). He sees me now, it all over. Good bi—

—BUSHNELL FALLS 3

Mike + Scott hiked in to the lean-to in the morning after spending the night in the parking lot of the Garden. After a strenuous day of hiking the yellow trail up to Marcy we drank much wine. Then the sounds started. In the night we heard some beastly roars. It didn't sound like anything I've ever heard before. Shortly we heard a woman scream. We thought it must be someone else having a little fun, but soon we heard what sounded like bones crunching and flesh tearing. It must be our imagination we thought, till we heard that beastly roar again. Mike decided to investigate. He took his knife and ventured out.

Twenty minutes of quiet went by, then I heard another scream "Nooooooo—" Then I heard that bone crunching again. I sat in the corner with my knife listening to heavy footsteps coming closer. This is it I thought. It came around the corner and it was only Mike with 2 blondes and a case of beer.

—BUSHNELL FALLS 1

The tall tales genre includes various impersonations. D.B. Cooper, Elvis, and various early nineteenth-century woodsmen make regular appearances, as do modern celebrities.

Well it's not too bad up here in upstate New York—not as good as the Ozarks but then again, they're in Missouri and that's God's country. Seems even here in the backwoods I'm still surrounded by gosh-darn New York liberals, but it sure

As I Glance through this log I notice many hikers are coming from southern New York and other states. I live in upstate New York, saratoga to be exact, Visiting the High Peaks region is an integral part of my life.

THAT AIN'T UPSTATE!

is nice when they're not around. I packed 3 nights worth of Big Macs for my stay—may need to go to Ticonderoga and get more—depends on how many I have for breakfast tomorrow.

The rocks in the pond are nice; you should give them to Pat Buchanan—I hear he wants to build himself a stone mansion in Tuscaloosa or something. The ore reserves beneath this pond are probably quite plentiful—this would make a magnificent quarry. Maybe make a dam between this and little Rock Pond because little Rock Pond is ugly. Besides, Little Rock is where Bill Clinton came from. The dam would provide hydroelectric power for the lumber mill. There'd be less room for feminazis and gays to have unprotected sex in. It's too damn cold and there's no television. Ditto! Ditto! Sincerely, Flush Lameblob Cape Girardildeau, Mizzeri.
—ROCK POND

A recurring class of entries purports to demonstrate very poor woodsmanship indeed.

Tonight we plan to burn down this lean-to & toast hotdogs while littering the lake with beer cans & roach clips. Also free base coke off our Coleman stove and fire off a few rounds with our 75 round clips on the AK-47 semi-automatic machine gun. It just rained yesterday, so our plan to burn down a couple thousand acres of Adirondack Forest was thwarted for now! After taking a nice swim & pollut-

ing the lake with pert-plus & Dove soap we decided the best way to piss you people off would be to declare Pharaoh Lake a waste water sewer treatment plant for N.Y. City—and a nuclear waste dumping site for 3 mile Island. Then we plan to clear the forest & make it a big shopping mall, amusement park, & trailer park …
—PHARAOH LAKE

This entry is from some friendly Vikings.

Because we're already out of Wild Turkey, and we have no acid rock to take us through, we will spend the evening denying our deepening fears of ravenous chipmunks, gargantuan killer bears and that putrid outhouse up the trail. Ingrid has been twice consumed by that murderous brook in full-pack attire. Hans, however, has recently reassembled her and she is still responsible for carrying her own load. (After reassembly, we decided to consume the leftover parts hastily before she noticed).

We are in search of the five gorgeous Frenchmen whom were here around the 27th or 28th. We number 7, 2 guys and 5 very attractive and voluptuous women (ranging 17–40) (two 17-yr.-olds, one 18- yr.-old, one 30-yr.-old and one 40-yr.-old). We are lounging about in our lederhosen and hand knit wool undergarments. Hans and Sven have intimidated the insects into submission. Ingrid, Helga and I (Gretchen) prepared a filling and satisfying meal of pickled herring, pumpernickel bread, reindeer jerky and gooseberry juice. Hans' yodeling has only attracted the attention of one horny yak and various other smaller animals. Olga and Ursula find their convalescence to be a worthy excuse for not gathering firewood or pumping water.

Jokim, our dog, has failed to impress us with his vocabulary during the trip. He seems to have become withdrawn and wanders listlessly, only occasionally muttering an ambiguous "voof" or two. Olga is failing fast due to her advanced age and this is known to be her last journey before her final venture to be a sewing woman in Valhalla. Because of her love of the mountains she has willed it that we leave here a piece of her heritage, a piece of her past. Thus, we have placed in the ziplock a spoon of questionable origin in her memory. So, use it with care and respect.

Although we find this lean-to empty, it simply does not compare to our god-covered home in our Nordic native land. As compared to the land of the midnight sun, it is becoming incredibly dark here and the Elders need to retire. We wish you the best of luck in all of your endeavors, and may some-day we meet on the grassy, open battlefields in the sky.
—BUSHNELL FALLS 3

Finally, this Adirondack chestnut.

We watched a red squirrel trying to get to a rock in the middle of the stream. It was too far to jump so he went out on an overhanging limb and dropped down on the rock. He got the beech nut that was on the rock. After he ate the nut he tried to jump back on the limb but it had sprung back up out of his reach. So as we were watching to see what his next move would be, a huge fish jumped out of the water and cleaned the poor squirrel right off the rock. We all agreed that seeing that was worth the trip here. About five minutes later Jim yelled at us that the fish was putting another nut on the rock.
—COLD RIVER 4

7

Let's Party!

Three days and no beer and I'm still alive …
—WALLFACE

FOR A SIGNIFICANT PART of the population, camping out means a party. Lean-tos close to a road have long served as party spots. In fact, any lean-to within a mile or so of vehicle access is almost always trashed. I wonder if shelters that are *very* close to a road are *less* trashed because they host a higher proportion of keggers, as opposed to the traditional can-and-bottle party. Party lean-tos are easily discerned by their high volume of garbage, half-chopped trees for many yards surrounding, and the prevalence of motorcycle and 4-wheeler tracks. The truly resourceful manage to drive their truck or SUV equivalent all the way to the lean-to, thus expanding exponentially the noise-making, beer-drinking, and mess-creation possibilities. Lean-tos accessible by motorized boat are plagued by the same problem.

Upon reaching the Boquet River
My body did nothing but shiver
The hash browns and pork
Did not seem to work
But man did that vodka deliver.

—BOQUET RIVER

Not everyone who brings booze on a camping trip becomes destructive. Some are simply worried that their supply holds out.

9/28 Arrived from B'ville, N.Y. to do a "little" early bow hunting. Almost alone in whole State Forest. Very few canoes (2 to be exact!) Perfect, perfect weather. Staying here at shelter till Sunday. Beer supply good.

9/29 Lots and lots of game here this year. Freekin' Dave rowed up and got a huge deer. Everybody has seen deer; well almost everybody. Perfect weather again. 60's and 70's. Beer supply OK.

9/30 Another awesome day. 70's lots of canoes today, why Craig even surprised a couple "topless" lady canoers (really!) ahhh that mountain air! Beer supply is holding up well, but Dr. McGillicutty has disappeared forever. Still seeing deer, well almost everybody is!

10/1 Late night getting close to solid foods again, just enough Bud for the row out. Perfect day even better than others. We've decided to send for more beer, and stay here for good. Just waiting for those two topless canoeists to come back down from High Falls. Life is good.
—CAGE LAKE SPRINGHOLE

Not everyone who enjoys a cold beverage (or something stronger) now and then is necessarily a party animal. However, along with the lack of a hot shower and a soft bed, alcohol deprivation ranks as one of camping's greatest hardships.

We didn't bring enough alcohol and dad spilled the scotch on the lean-to floor. We had to stop my brother from getting on his hands and knees and licking up the remaining drops.
—PHARAOH LAKE 5

Unfortunately for all but the thirstiest, the weight limitations inherent in backpacking make hauling significant quantities of beer impractical. Gourmets and the romantically inclined bring wine, but the bottles are heavy, and

there's something not quite right about allowing a nice Beaujolais to slosh around in a Nalgene bottle next to the bumwad in the bottom of your pack. That leaves hard liquor as the beverage of choice for the tippling trekker.

Another beautiful day. Cold last night, frost on the ground in the morning. Got drunk last night, drank all the booze. Going to get more we buried up here in the woods last time. Always prepared.
—NUMBER FOUR 2

Arrived late last night. Deer flies were horrendous. Made a fire, drank lots of whiskey, then passed out. Now we're passing on.
—GRIFFIN RAPIDS

Whiskey is reputed to have a powerful medicinal effect when taken properly, an opinion not unknown to the experienced woodsman: *Liquid pain killer for the aching joints. I think we all need it. Cascade Pond.*

Not all of the attitude adjustment is centered on alcohol. One occasionally detects the unmistakable odor of marijuana wafting on a campground breeze. Forest rangers seem to follow a lenient confiscate-rather-than-arrest policy when encountering such use. However, even this relative tolerance is not appreciated by all.

What a relaxing few days it has been out here. It's nice to get away after a long semester at school. It would've been even better but a policeman came and confiscated our recreation this morning. I personally think that was a crime. Myself, along with 3 of my childhood friends planned this getaway a few weeks ago while still at school. After a week of finals we just needed to separate from society for a while.

We had 1 1/2 cases of beer and some home grown stuff to smoke, kind stuff. We took care of all garbage and empty cans. And we're not making much noise, other than a Grateful Dead CD playing on low.

What I'm trying to say is we were peaceful, and considerate of the environment. So why did he have to bother us? Luckily he didn't find the Bacardi. I'm just upset he bothered us at all. There are many more atrocities happening than 4 guys sipping on a few beers, smoking a few bowls, and relaxing. I think Ranger Danger could find something better to do.
—CASCADE POND

MAN IS IT COLD !

WHERE ARE THE BEARS? TIME to BRAVE ON TO THE NEXT LEAN-TO !

On the Appalachian Trail there is a tradition in which "trail angels" leave coolers full of goodies alongside the path for thru hikers to discover and consume. The fortunate find the lucky cooler containing a six-pack. At some lean-tos, tradition holds that each visitor leave some flavor of alcoholic beverage in the nearby "beer stump." If there is no stump, other locations will do.

We left two bottles of fine French chardonnay in the spring behind the lean-to. Here's hoping Joe [the lean-to adopter] will encourage this behavior as part of the lean-to creed. P.S. carry out the bottles after you've enjoyed the wine.
—GRIFFIN RAPIDS

The next occupants evidently did enjoy the present.

Hi everybody and thanks, the wine was great! But Fred fell

out of his canoe and now I think he caught hypothermia.
—GRIFFIN RAPIDS

For those so inclined, a similar practice applies to other substances.

I have left a gift for the next traveler who wants it, a hand carved "Adirondack" pipe filled with home-grown Northern Lights cared for by my sister and blessed with the love of Jah and the Goddess. If this is not your thing, please leave for someone who will enjoy it with love. Check the red coffee can on the shelf and enjoy. It may be the catalyst that opens you to an incredible experience.
—BIG SHALLOW

Perhaps the best way to end this chapter is with that drinking tradition, a toast. The set-up, for those not up to speed on their Adirondack hermits, concerns Noah John Rondeau, a famous recluse who for more than 40 years lived deep in the Cold River country between Long Lake and Lower Saranac Lake. The remains of his hermitage can be found through a careful search, but only after a walk of some nineteen miles on the Northville–Placid Trail.

Walked from Raquette and Cold to Rondeau Camp. Trail could use some work, but not bad. Also raised a can of the amber nectar and saluted with that famous Polish Toast: Yo Rondeau, Nice Driveway.
—OULUSKA PASS

8

What a Mess

Have you done the "funny walk" before leaving? Walk around the campsite with head down looking for scraps of trash—thread, bits of foil, plastic, etc.
—GRIFFIN RAPIDS

THE LOGICAL RESULT of many of the activities reported in the previous chapter is the trashed lean-to. Unfortunately, they are all too common. Reading a few of these accounts is enough to make you want to stay home.

Herschey and I both decided that we hiked enough for today. Strolled over from Carry L.T. which is a scum pit with trash all over the place. Cigarette butts all over shore and in river, a Styrofoam cooler with an old pair of sneakers inside the L.T., a garbage bag full of trash just off in the woods. Some old spaghetti in the field. Enough black flies to suck the blood off a Woolly Mammoth within minutes. What a hellhole.
—STEPHENS POND

It's true; for some reason, trashed lean-tos *do* attract more bugs.

In the fall, hunters sometimes outfit lean-tos with a variety of gear in an attempt to create a backwoods cabin. What's mainly needed to convert a lean-to to a cabin is a fourth wall, a modification usually undertaken with plastic sheeting.

First time adopters making initial clean-up trip. A "garbage pit" unlike its usual well kept condition. Enough industrial grade plastic and duct tape to indicate an apparent but aborted attempt to fabricate a pool cover for Blueberry Pond!
—NUMBER FOUR 1

Truly messy lean-tos attract the most vehement screeds found in the registers. A typical example:

The pig people were here. They've been just about every-where in this lovely wilderness. They are like dogs, dribbling their piss wherever they go. You always know by the stink and garbage left behind that they've been here. The others, who knows how many, pass through quietly, leaving not a trace, not a ripple. I hate the pig people, for without a thought they will poison the earth.

But there is room for hope, for it does seem to me that there is less pig sign scattered about this year then there was last. We are all growing and changing and if we wish, the sky's the limit. Who knows what can happen. A self-aware pig is not a pig at all.
—STEPHENS POND

A standard lean-to feature is graffiti, either carved into the wood itself or inscribed with a charcoal stick. *Graffiti is reaching a new peak in terms of the depth of the inci-sions. The lean-to may collapse from initials alone!* Fish Pond 1.

The standard topics: who was here and when; who loves who; vulgarities.

*I don't mind graffiti on the walls. I mind its lack of origi-
nality. Your name and date, oh boy! How about a quote or
a drawing? Be creative!*
—OULUSKA PASS

A graffiti subject ubiquitous to lean-tos near water is the
fishing take. Many a lakeside shelter is adorned with charcoal accounts of brook trout catches—numbers, lengths,
weights. As a fisherman I have attempted to verify the information found in these postings. In fact, on several occa-
sions I made fishing trips based solely on such endorsement as *Jim and Dave, 13 brook trout, 5/18/97* scrawled on
a log wall. I will not divulge the findings of my research,
other than to say that I am not as offended as others at the
presence of these messages.

Leaving food waste in or around the lean-to ranks with
graffiti and trash disposal as a wilderness *faux pas.*
However, as the next entry points out, it isn't just thoughtless and disgusting; there can be larger consequences.

*Only saw one party a "gentleman" & four young
boys (early teens I estimate). Saw them at Wolf
Lake outlet crossing. To my horror upon my return
to camp at the lean-to they had eaten lunch in my
camp and had discarded Vienna Weiner cans &
other smelly stuff in the fireplace. Some looked like military
rations. Pretty thoughtless behavior in bear country. If I
were in the grizzly country of Montana I would have chased
them down & had them arrested after I got out.*
    *Reckless endangerment—felony could be charged. I went
through great trouble to keep a clean site since I did not
want a bear tearing up the place while I was gone. That
idiot did not know how long I planned to be gone—could
have been all day.*
    Also I presume one of the little bastards stole my flash-

light. I had deliberately left it next to my sleeping bag & even thought for a moment I should stow it away before leaving for a day hike—decided that anyone this far back would be decent & never endanger the life of another by stealing vital equipment and supplies. This too could be a reckless endangerment charge especially if food, medical supplies or shelter were stolen. I guess I should calm down since this was just a case of mild adult stupidity and juvenile delinquency. Not enough to start shooting over.
—COWHORN POND

The entry above allows us to digress to the subject of theft. Although rare, it happens, as discussed in this entry.

Now a word of warning. On our way hiking in from Wanakena, we had a disappointing experience. Upon reaching Cowhorn Junction, I set my pack down so I could help my wife up the hill with hers. I was gone no more than 10 minutes. On our way up the hill, we passed four boys ages 10–14. We said "hello" and went on our way. When we reached the top, we discovered my pack, contents strewn about. It appeared that nothing of value was taken, short of a Zip-lock bag full of trail mix. In their haste to open the pack, they cut a bungee cord (with a knife, it would appear).

I wish this incident could be attributed to an animal, but when was the last time you saw a bear pass up raw steaks for a package of hard, dried fruit? I digress…shortly after we found the pack, an adult and three other youths came along, part of the previous group of kids. The 'trailmaster' denied that his boys would do anything like that (the kids with him didn't seem to agree). If this whole affair wasn't bad enough, the Zip-loc baggie was left lying beside the trail (my wife had spotted it halfway up the hill). I hope this isn't indicative of what all campers have in store.
—COWHORN POND

Happily, the majority are conscientious hikers who carry out what they carry in. Lean-to adopters, trail crews, and Good Samaritans do their part to clean up the messes made by others. This sort of entry is found in nearly every register.

To Adirondack Mtn Club: I have been coming to these woods and ponds for nearly 20 years, and they are my spiritual home. The only disappointment in being here was having to see how awful the shelters were. Now that disappointment is gone, thanks to the volunteer efforts of the ADK and probably others, which are an inspiration to all of us campers to clean up. Now, instead of cringing to the aftermath of Woodstock around each shelter, my heart warms at the sight of a lonely butt or twist tie, because now I know it is finally worth it to carry these tiny traces of civilization back home.
—GRIFFIN RAPIDS

9

I'm Tired and I Wanna Go Home

We came, we saw, we need a shower and our MTV.
—HAMILTON STREAM

I
T'S NOT ALL HAPPY TRAILS out there. Crummy weather, bug attacks, blisters, bad food, the smell of unwashed bodies … Tell me again: Why do we do this? Backpacking to remote places necessarily involves foregoing creature comforts, an unhappy fact for some.

How I ever let someone talk me into doing this I'll never figure out. Came from N.Y.C. and have never been so bored in my entire life. Nothing to do! What only activity I had fizzled when the battery in my laptop went dead. Bugs, flies, mice, rain and no restaurants. THIS SUCKS! I can't wait to get home.
—OXSHOE POND

The "nothing to do here" theme recurs with surprising frequency.

I will never go on a dumb hike like this again. What's the sense of it? There's just as much beauty at my house way out in the country. It hasn't been that bad so far but I know it's gonna' get much worse! I mean, what are you gonna' get

out of this climb but exercise?
—BOQUET RIVER

For others, the problem is the presence of the sort of people writing in the preceding entries.

Group of seven in from Durant for fishing weekend. Stayed at Cascade first night. Fishing isn't very good. Saw a coyote chase a big 8 pt. buck into the lake this morning. He swam up the shoreline and crossed the lake, ran up the hill and crossed the trail. Saw two otters and big beaver yesterday. Nice place but we won't be back. Too many Flatlanders running around. Lakes are dying and fished out. Have to go places the Flatlanders don't know about. Out today and back to Gloversville.
—STEPHENS POND

A subset of the "bad trip" genre is the hauling along of a companion of the opposite sex with whom one doesn't quite see eye to eye.

We were here, beautiful day! Trying not to argue. He thinks I'm coming back to sleep over. Nice try! See you on another day trip.
—OXSHOE POND

Brought my sister, her first time in the Park. Didn't like it. Imagine that, my heaven, her hell. Go figure.
—MIDDLE SETTLEMENT LAKE

The lack of creature comforts is frequently noted.

Glad trip home will be downstream. All in all a great experience. Glad I came. Although I think my next trip will be at a place with a name like Hilton or Sheraton. I miss maid service.
—HIGH FALLS EAST

One of the primary reasons for an unpleasant backpacking experience is blisters. I should know. My first extended trip, covering seventeen days on the Appalachian Trail, was undertaken in a pair of primitive Vasque boots made of a grade of leather so stiff and unsupple that it is often substituted for deck plating in the world's less demanding navies. My feet bled pretty much every step of the way, an experience that is by no means unique.

Day Six on the N–P Trail. We are currently experiencing our first protracted period of non-rain, strange concept this blue sky following the past five days of gray. Heading to Duckhole for the last evening on the trail. Our poor, blistered, sore, scraped, beaten, soaked down-trodden feet will always rue the day we set out on this journey. Borrowing my brothers 1/2 size too small Wilderness 2 hiking boots was a major blunder not soon to be forgotten. The scars on my feet will bear testament for a long time to come. Luckily for my feet the boots have found a useful place dangling from the back of my pack since I have been hiking with my Teva sandals the past couple days!
—OULUSKA PASS

Some of the most amusing entries cover bad trips in a group context. Maybe the reason misery loves company is because there are more people to whom you can complain.

We've been on the trail since Monday, July 24 at Cedarlands Scout Reservation. We've canoed most of the way but we've had many carries and more to go. We started in Upper Saranac Lake. We camped the first night at Polliwog Pond. On the second day on our way to Long Pond J. A. & his son flipped their canoes. They were ok, just wet. S. G. at the end of the carry to Floodwood Pond from Middle Pond, was attacked by a wasp nest and was stung. So WATCH OUT.

And then it rained and it seemed like it could get no worse but it did. We couldn't find a camp. We ended up camping off the side of the canoe carry to Long Pond. When we went to bed our utensils and pots were licked clean by raccoons and chipmunks. Earlier in the day our guide sent us the wrong way twice and attempted to feed 2 chipmunks but the chipmunks decided to bite his finger.

When we woke up today it was raining still but we continued our 1½ mile canoe carry to be attacked by wasps once again. But we finally made it to this lean-to. We went for a swim out to the rocks and back and J. G. and S. had leaches on them. So WATCH OUT again!!! This lean-to is like a high priced hotel compared to what we've been through. Boy Scout Troop 354.

We Saw this in the lake

Be carfull

—FISH PONDS 1

I can't wait to hike out tomorrow. We have been out here for five days, and I'm getting kind of tired of this wilderness stuff. Oh, well.

The first day was really bad. We hiked into Wanika Falls with 40 pound Gama packs (I weigh 85 pounds!) and when we got to W. Falls, the lean to was so terrible! We put down our sleeping bags, and went up Street and Nye. But, we couldn't get up due to lack of time and a huge downpour. So, we came back down to find that our sleeping bags were soaked because the roof had leaked! It was terrible!

We slept that night very wet, and then the next day we conquered Street and Nye. Then we hiked to Duck Hole and arrived at about 8:30 PM. The next day we slacked and swam, then we came to Ward Brook, all nine of us, to find ONE person in the lean to. Well, we went to the camping spot and spent the night there while getting rained on at night.

We woke up and we only did Seward, because of cold weather, and now we are here, instead of next to that lady. She was so mean! She even had a hammock that she hung up while we were dying (well, not really). We don't like her very much, but we will not kill her when we next see her. Some people!

Tomorrow, we will go back to our camp without electricity, TV's, candy, radios, where we have to get up at 6:45 AM, where we do a lot of work, but we love it! (Camp, not the work!) I can't wait until I see my friends at camp!
—Number Four 1

It's been said that families are the source of our greatest joy and our greatest misery. This is as true in the woods as anywhere else.

Hello, this is a great campsite if you like bugs. Me and my whole family was excited when we found a campsite with a lean-to, a toilet, a nice fireplace and a journal that we could spend our time reading/writing in. We had to race another group of people to get this campsite. We beat them, so they ended up searching the lake for a different campsite. They found an empty one across the lake. It also has a lean-too, but it isn't as good of a campsite as this one.

I'm a little disappointed because I read the rest of the journal and it seems like everyone else has had a more interesting stay here. The only thing I've seen so far is the chipmunk. I haven't seen the bear, raccoon, woodpecker, or owl. We haven't even caught a fish. We haven't even gotten any bites. Tomorrow we have to make a big portage from Nellie Pond to Long Lake. I'm definitely not looking forward to that. It seems like we do more portaging than canoeing.

The outfitter said that part of the portage tomorrow is going to be flooded because they've had a lot of rain around here recently. We'll have to walk barefoot through that part of the portage. The problem with swimming at this campsite is that if while your swimming you have the need to put your feet on the ground they get stuck in the mud. Overall this campsite is pretty good, it's no paradise, but hey that's not why we came camping any way. We came to rough it for a little while, to get away from civilization, or just because someone made you go with them (e.g.: a parent).

At least this campsite is better than the rest of them. I am thankful that everyone who visited this campsite before me kept it clean. It's a great place to visit but I sure wouldn't want to live here.
—FISH POND 1

Finally there are the just-plain-bad trips, as well as the just-plain bad-tempered. We'll conclude this chapter with an example of each.

Yesterday we all traveled from the inlet to here and now we are aching pretty bad. Last night we heard something two-legged stomping behind this shelter. Not to mention something growling. Not only that but then we couldn't sleep for the rest of the night. We probably didn't get more than an hours sleep. There were rodents crawling through our food all night, even after we chased them away several times. Also, does anyone else hear the pounding that sounds like thunder back in the mountain? We heard it all night and still this morning. At this point I don't know if we'll make it to the High Falls. Five of us want to go home and one insists we move onward.
—GRIFFIN RAPIDS

I will never come back to this God forsaken Seward Range. The flies suck, the rain sucks, the brush sucks, the two hour long mile sucks and the guidebook sucks with descriptions such as "there will be a mossy rock to your right."
—NUMBER FOUR 1

10

Weather

Here's a weather tip from Bill: "If you can see the mountains, it's just about to rain. If you can't, it already is."
—*WARD BROOK*

THE WEATHER IS THE ONE THING that can make or break a camping trip. Although there are a lot of entries commenting on "what a beautiful day it is," all of the interesting weather-related entries are about bad weather and the misery it brings. On rainy days there is no view and you are often cold and miserable. This is the time when the lean-to is most appreciated, a dry haven from the elements.

Back again
Full moon boom'n down
Little raggedy clouds fly'n high and wild
It's a ghost riders kinda' night
And sure as I'm alive
It's a night to be out

—*STREETER LAKE*

Arrived here soaking wet and tired from boots being full of water late Friday 23rd. Came in the long way via High Falls up through Pine Ridge. Rained most of the way in Friday. It rained Sat. night, Sun. night, Mon. morning and Mon. night from 9 p.m. and is still raining now 9 a.m. Tue. Why did the weatherman have to be right about this week?

Rained so hard last night it was impossible to sleep. Left my metal frame tent with the foil insulating blanket underneath for the safety of the lean-to twice when the thunderstorms rolled thru. When I got up at 6 a.m. I almost expected to see animals lined up in pairs waiting to board my inflatable raft.

—*COWHORN POND*

It was wet. Amazingly, unbelievable, incredibly, mind-bogglingly wet. And I got very wet as well. Our adventure began as a dry sunny morning. The trail wasn't too hard until we got 2/3's of the way up Emmons. At first it was just a low rumble in the distance. It slowly increased until it hovered over our heads. It was big and dark. Its dark puffy eyes seemed to pinpoint each one of us. It was … the raincloud. From then on our trip was miserable. As I charged through a puddle of mud and gush, I heard mom saying, "I think Margaret is going to need new shoes for school." When we finally got back dripping wet and muddy I stripped down and hopped into my dry clothes and stayed in the lean-to until I had to pee the next morning. That night we all seemed to look at dad as if to say, "I can't believe you made us do that!"

We were going to do another mountain today, but since it's raining we're just going to pack out. But that means I'll have to put on my shoes, which don't look too inviting.
—Blueberry

During bad weather, lean-tos fill up, and unspoken rules about giving each other space are forgotten. They become social centers where hikers gather to share news and stories while they watch the sky drain. They can, however, get a bit crowded.

The most exciting thing to happen this afternoon, besides spending close quarters with five dirty, wet bodies and one very wet, smelly dog was sleet! Yes sleet … in August … who would figure? Thank God it was short lived.
—Hamilton Stream

As the next entries testify, rain presents particular problems for those near a stream.

Last night I pity anyone in a tent as the heavens opened up with a deluge for half the night. Me, being the hip woodsman, hung my food near the river, all the time thinking, "hey, it's really gonna' rain tonight." When I awoke the Cold River resembled a molten river of white. It had rose two feet—covering all the boulders in the river. And my food? It was hung over a cascade a good five yards from the shore. What a night and what a sight—the Cold River in wrath. Full moon tonight and the river is still a froth of white water which lights up like liquid metal.
—COLD RIVER 4

It is now 6 p.m. We arrived at 1:30 p.m. The river has risen 20+ inches. But for saving room at the launch site for future paddlers, our canoe would be halfway to Inlet by now. At 7:30 we find the canoe securely tied to a stout tree and the river 4" higher.

Dawn 10/22 revealed the river in flood. The canoe was upside down in 3' of water. The stump at the top of the falls was surrounded by the torrent. The moral to this story is that when it rains for 22 out of 24 hrs, this river will rise 5 feet. We're stranded here until tomorrow.

10/23 River is still very high but appears navigable. We still feel like Noah.
—HIGH FALLS EAST

If you do survive the bugs and the mud and the rain does finally stop and you do get to the top of the mountain, you will find … well, here's what you might find.

While my companions vainly attempt to lift their spirits with "rat-a-tui" and grape juice, I am more pessimistic. I have traveled to the High Peaks region 3 times now and still never witnessed the spectacular views everyone raves about.

I'm beginning to believe a conspiracy is involved. The trails do not lead to the top of Mt. Marcy but rather in a circle with landmarks matching those on the map. The ever-present fog fools people into believing they are really at the top of the mountain. Thus, people from all over faithfully return to spend their tourist dollars in hopes of climbing Marcy on a clear day.

If people only walked past the bogus boundary marked "re-vegetation zone" I'm sure they would find some two-bit flunky named "Vinny" operating a special effects/fog machine similar to the one in the "Wizard of Oz"!
—BUSHNELL FALLS 3

Not everybody complains though.

Brought my journalist pal from England ... marginal weather, but as pal's from London, he thinks its just fine.
—BIG SHALLOW

In the pre-dawn hours of July 15, 1995, a microburst—a type of violent storm with severe downdraft winds—cut a swath through the northwest and central Adirondacks. The storm claimed five lives, among them several campers killed by falling trees, and caused millions of dollars in property damage. Nearly one million acres were affected. Seven hundred miles of trail were closed (some for two years), and eighty-five campsites damaged. The Five Ponds Wilderness was the area hardest hit.

There are a handful of entries from campers who were in lean-tos in the Five Ponds Wilderness during the storm. They, and those who visited soon afterward, expressed amazement that no lean-tos had been destroyed. *The lean-to is intact under a stack of trees* and *amazing that nobody was killed* are typical entries. The entries of those who were present during the storm express the extent to which the world went haywire. This account is from a ten-year-old girl.

Last night was a big rush to get to bed. We woke up at 5:00 a.m. in the morning and zipped the flies on our tents. It rained like crazy. Then the wind started. It almost blew our tents over! Trees fell all around us, and there was lightening everywhere. The campsite is a mess this morning, and the skeeters are ruthless, and the chipmunks are attacking. We are leaving now, we hope to reach Inlet today.
—GRIFFIN RAPIDS

Another one.

Storm hit area last night and did it catch us by surprise! We scrambled to cover the opening of the lean-to, and everything got soaked! High winds knocked down almost all of the huge trees beside the water and one partially hit the lean-to! By morning the sun was out and everything was calm. Fishing! Hiking! Cook outs! Swimming! Braving the storm! Trees falling! Getting soaked! Freezing! What an adventure!

P.S. The outhouse bit the dust in the storm last night. So break out the shovel.
—BIG SHALLOW

One more, this time a before-and-after entry.

Last night I paddled up Buck Brook to the main Beaver Pond. It's a very tight and shallow excursion with many obstacles including six dams. Today was a vigorous bushwack over to the abandoned yellow trail & then off to Buck Pond. The old trail is pretty easy to follow—being well marked with blazes & many old markers. Getting over to it was the hard part! To those who pass, take time to enjoy the beavers as they swim back and forth or the shrews as they hop about the lean-to. Enjoy this great place! And after you swat that deerfly, take a moment to recycle them through the minnows below.

Last night's violent thunderstorm has changed this site forever. We lost over a dozen trees to the storm's high winds. The ground is littered with branches and fallen giants, several of which now block our canoe's path down river. We'll have to carry around this mess. Even a corner of our lean-to is damaged. Luckily we're OK after spending an hour watching bolts of lightening, driving rain, and wind gusts that brought these trees crashing down around us.
—CAGE LAKE SPRINGHOLE

Immediately afterward DEC forest rangers helicoptered to the Five Ponds to ascertain the damage and rescue stranded canoers and hikers. There are several hurriedly scribbled entries reporting their author's rescue and asking others to respect their gear, which was necessarily left behind. Several other entries show up a week or two later from campers returning for their gear. At least one person's disappeared.

Granted permission by the local rangers to enter the Five Ponds area, as it is being closed to public, for the reason of rescuing stranded canoes left by a party evacuated by chopper. We are sad at the loss of such an enchanting forest, but Mother Nature knows its own motives. Most likely we'll be the last ones here for a while. Respect the woods.
—BIG SHALLOW

But they weren't the last visitors for a while. The immediate aftermath was viewed by a surprising number of trekkers, many of whom (known colloquially as "forest gnomes") defied DEC's closure order and brought saws and axes to clear the way. These entries, arranged in chronological order beginning a week later, illustrate the incredible power of the storm.

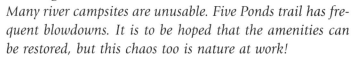

Day trip from camp-site 22 (5 Ponds Trail) by canoe. No sign of visitors to High Falls on Monday. River in flood. Navigation hazardous due to a number of blowdowns forming dangerous strainers. The massive destruction throughout the wilderness from the storm of one week ago is awesome to behold. Many river campsites are unusable. Five Ponds trail has frequent blowdowns. It is to be hoped that the amenities can be restored, but this chaos too is nature at work!
—GRIFFIN RAPIDS

Arrived Wed. 8/2 from Inlet, amazed at storm damage but even more amazed today after paddle to High Falls. Many trees blocking river, some you can get around and many you have to lift over. Thank goodness we left camp gear here at #36. Would never have made it if canoes full. In places forest looks as though bomb went off at 50' of elevation, topping trees over large area. Don't know how many sites were occupied night of storm but amazing anyone survived.
—GRIFFIN RAPIDS

Party of six canoed from Inlet. This is my 5th year camping in this region and I couldn't recognize a single landmark on the entire river. High Rock campsite—one of my favorites, is totally devastated. As for here at High Falls, I didn't realize I was anywhere near the falls until I saw them. The destruction is unbelievable. I hope the area is cleared to make hiking possible again even though the land is "Forever Wild." This is a very special area to me and I hate to see it in this condition. I hope to bring my kids here someday to show them how beautiful the world can be.
—HIGH FALLS EAST

After passing a bit of beaver swamp followed by a brook crossing, at a point we estimated to be quite close to the intersection with the Buck Pond Trail, we encountered a vast section of difficult blowdown. Having run out of time, we turned around, because believe me it would take some time to get through that next piece. I suggest leaving early if you want to undertake this. Once you arrive at the impressive blowdown area it will be necessary to either proceed with compass bearing or to station one person at the last known spot while the other crawls around trying to find where it goes ...

I'm a little worried about the remaining leaning white pine behind the lean-to; concerned that a North wind could drop it into the most obvious tent site around (where in fact our tent is). Being up here and seeing the massive trees dropped across tent sites is one of the most frightening things I've ever seen.
—CAGE LAKE SPRINGHOLE

Up early today and packed canoe for upstream adventure. Was surprised to make the Robinson River so quickly—thanks to those with saws! Was able to paddle over two beaver dams due to the high water (new green grass about a foot under the surface). Had to haul over another dam with a rope. Continued up river, hauling around one blowdown and a cut-into log that the canoe just wouldn't fit under. I believe I paddled off the Five Ponds topo map until the blowdowns were too thick to pass. A fast float back and happy to see this shelter still empty. Full of warm food and happy now.
—GRIFFIN RAPIDS

Above Camp Johnny is where the blowdown is most intense. Expect to navigate a fallen tree every 25–50 yards. The right side of the swamp took the greatest hit here. The only breaks that one sees are when the river meanders to the left

side of the swamp. High Falls is still beautiful, and it appears that the river is navigable as far as one might care to go. However, a 20-inch saw might be a nice insurance policy.
—GRIFFIN RAPIDS

After the storm, a vigorous debate ensued as to what should be done with all the downed timber. *So much for the microburst, I call it a megablast! Let the logging begin (if not what a waste of resources), Cage Lake Springhole,* is a typical entry in a theme that recurs often in the fall of 1995. The registers contain debates over how the logging should be done. *If you could log this place by helicopter, then you wouldn't have to put logging roads all over this pristine place to get all the wood laying all over. Skidders would wreck the whole valley. Cage Lake Springhole.* Others warn of the fire danger. But state policy prohibits logging on Wilderness lands, and the warned-of fire has yet to occur.

Left to its own, trails and canoe routes cleared to allow visitors, the Five Ponds has begun the process of regeneration, a process perhaps best recognized by those who have been around long enough to witness the changes nature brings.

Some friends and I are coming here for deer season and I always love to come to Oswegatchie country summer and winter, so I can give them a report of the devastation of their favorite sites. I'll not live another 70 years to see nature restore what the storm destroyed, but it will be restored if we humans don't succeed in killing the planet.
—CAGE LAKE SPRINGHOLE

he has to be a heck of an acrobate
to get our bag of peanuts.
We will keep you tuned for more
information.

step ①

peanuts

14 feet

20 feet

step ②   What the bear has to do

step ③

11

Critters

We saw so much wildlife, the place is just full of living things. Beavers working all night long. Frogs peeping, a heron that landed right near the bank. Three different kinds of hawks, maybe a turkey vulture, bunnies and a deer—sounds like the set of Bambi, doesn't it?
—CAGE LAKE SPRINGHOLE

THE GREATEST NUMBER OF ENTRIES in the registers is devoted to critters, and bears are by far the most popular topic. The Adirondack bruin is the black bear, a generally shy and retiring species given to berry picking, mushroom gathering, and other such solitary pursuits in the deep woods. Contrary to what some believe, a black bear will almost never act aggressively towards a human. Your most common view, if you are lucky enough to see one at all, is of its comical back end bounding into the woods.

Friday evening I came face to face with a bear on the Calkins Creek Road at dusk. He and I came to an agreement as to who had the right of way. I breathlessly waited in silence as he ambled by, then catching my scent at last, he took off up the hillside. Honestly, 300+ lbs. A bear on the run always seems to me to defy all of the laws of physics—there is nothing faster. Astonished that I met the bear less than 1/4 mile from where I had a similar encounter 2 years ago. They must have runways like deer.
—COLD RIVER 4

Bears are smart, and a more likely explanation is that it had learned that the road provided easy going. Bears have learned to make use of humans in other ways. In this, they have always reminded me of Labrador retrievers: basically good-natured, but they will do anything for food.

Food-stealing bears are the stuff of legend in the High Peaks. Some operatives are well known to rangers, caretakers, and other regular visitors, having developed a signature M.O. Over the course of a season, the resident bear will return to rifle food sacks from the same lean-to every night. Even the most expert attempt at hanging food is defeated by these forest masterminds. In certain areas, entire registers are devoted exclusively to theft and loss prevention, for example this series from the High Peaks.

Black bear
Prowls at midnight
Through moon-bright birch

—*KLONDIKE*

Stayed near here up the hill in a tent, but shared in the excitement when a large 400 lb. hungry bear came and swatted down a burlap bag of food belonging to a group of young fellows who were staying here. Eyewitness accounts say the bear clambered up twelve feet in seven seconds and stretched its arm out six feet to scratch open the sack. Later that night it ate all the food in two other hangs back up in the hills. Look for tell tale scratch marks on the trees. Hang high, far away from the trunk, and tie up high. Birch trees are best, pine too soft, too easy to climb. This bear is making a living off the tourist trade. Can be scared away with banging pans and throwing rocks.
—*CEDAR POINT*

We're from Deerfoot Lodge and we're up for three days. The bear tore down our burlap bag but only ate peas and carrots & hot chocolate. We were quite lucky. Last night the bear came for another visit. Nine of us were sleeping in this lean-to. I was the only one up—it was less than ten feet

away. It was huge! Had to be over 500 lbs. It tried to get into one of our Nalgenes with jug juice in it but was unsuccessful. Left claw marks on the bottle. Also tried to climb our bear bag tree—it failed!
—CEDAR POINT

Well, as promised, we were rudely visited by the bruin tonight. He swiped our grub at 10:15 p.m. and we lost all our gorp, Tang, breakfast oatmeal, and some of our freeze-dried. Lucky for us our lean-to mates, Seth and Mark, are leaving the woods tomorrow and have donated their extra food, assuming anything survives the night. The goddamn bears (there are two—we gave chase, and they came back to watch us retie the bag in the birch by the outhouse), are sure to be back.

Mike was just dozing off when he heard crackling, then our food came crashing down! I removed the rubber tip to my walking stick, and the hunt for the hairy beggar was on. Five headlamps crisscrossed thru the woods, and we quickly found their beady eyes, but too late.
—CEDAR POINT

Hello from Girl Scout Camp Glengarra. We started out on the 6th for a two-week journey. The first night we lost two bags of food to a rather large bear at Johns Brook. We stayed yet another day and lost another bag of food. This time we saw the bear. They look a lot smaller in the zoo.
—KLONDIKE

The standard defense calls for hanging food bags at a great height, well away from any tree. This entry describes the proper technique, as well as a back-up.

Put up five bear bags and our garbage all within site of the lean-to. Minimum 20' high and 8'–10' out from the trunk. We plan on eating well. Sorta' resembles the movie

"COMA" with so many things hanging. Contingency plan: If the bears show up for food we are going to sacrifice Richard.
—GRIFFIN RAPIDS

Others take a less conventional approach.

Hearing all the talk down at the landing about bears, we decided we needed to protect ourselves and our food. Where could we put 2 large coolers full of food? On the roof of the lean-to? No, too obvious. So we buried it in the sand at the foot of the bank. It took some doing. Andy worked for about an hour digging a hole big enough. It took all our efforts to carry them back down, wrap them in tarps and bury them again...Our evening continued with stories, songs and bear dances. Such fun. All this effort produced no bear.
—GRIFFIN RAPIDS

Other techniques:

Stopped for lunch on way from Sand Lake to Oswegatchie with daughter Sue. No problem with bears eating food; Sue beat them to it.
—WOLF POND

Bear is lulled to sleep by gently rubbing belly. Great warmth at night, but do not wear any cologne.
—LAKE COLDEN

The registers are an ongoing report of local conditions. When local conditions are crawling with bears, the registers offer helpful advice.

As far as bears go, please always remember and don't ever forget: leave all food out or put in tent. Bacon grease repels the black bears. Food scraps can be used as deterrents. If

you're not afraid, they won't come around.
—GRIFFIN RAPIDS

Needless to say, the bears have a different take, and on occasion they take the time to record their views.

Yo! Lissen' up! We sick an' tied o' yo' sheet wi' hangin' de food bags! Why don' you homeboys wise up some an leave us some food-fixed lest it get so's we don' hef't' come afte yo' whi' asses! De Black Bears. Ouluska Pass

Mr. Ranger Sir: I wish to complement you on your excellent lean-to! It is very nice to lure people here so I can eat their pic-a-nic baskets! Yogi Bear.
—OULUSKA PASS

After bears the most popular subjects are mice and chipmunks, also pests when it comes to the food bag.

There is this little chipmunk, he is quite a thief. You have only to be away from camp for 30 seconds & there he is in all your belongings. Or just lurking in the nearby bushes watching your every move. Especially watching for where you may hide your favorite cookies.
—O'NEIL FLOW

Where bears use brute force, the chippie relies on adorable antics. Not everyone is amused.

ATTN: BOUNTY HUNTERS: Bounty on one nasty chipmunk—years supply of gorp for his capture. Small, fat & likes hot chocolate, gorp and pop tarts! I'm off—don't believe anything they write about me.
—STEPHENS POND

The next entry:

O.K. she left approximately 1 hour ago. The table dancers and tables are being airlifted in. The D.J.'s are floating in from across the pond. If I only had guests—other than this monstrously well fed chipmunk.
—STEPHENS POND

Some spend a great deal of time trying to catch the little buggers. I used to frequent a lean-to in western Virginia that was absolutely crawling with mice. One trip, clever fellow that I am, I decided to bring mousetraps. I set up a pair next to the fireplace (yes, Virginia, lean-tos often have fireplaces) and one in each corner. It wasn't long before I heard a loud *snap* and found my first dead mouse. Then another and another. I spent the next hour busily clearing and re-baiting the traps, which never lacked for customers. A not-so-funny thing about mousetraps: They don't always kill cleanly. Sometimes they get just the tip of a nose or a paw. I ended up burning the traps in the fire.

Arrived yesterday around 4:00. There are quite a few mice up here! We set up a makeshift trap out of a pot, stick and piece of rope. We caught us a mouse! We let it go only to be awoken later by 3–4 of his buddies. They climbed into my pack, around the fire and also onto our sleeping bags as we tried to sleep.
—INLET FLOW

Others, knowing the danger, bring protection.

It has been a rough three days. I have protected my three human companions from all sorts of wild fierce animals. The chipmunks are all around but I have kept them at bay. It is a hard job but I don't mind because they feed me very well. Last night I had chili and spanish rice. One guy is

easy. I just give him my sad eye look and he will give me a morsel to nibble on. Got to go, I can hear a chipmunk. Shena (the dog).
—HAMILTON STREAM

Dogs appear frequently in the registers. The most interesting entries are crafted by canines themselves.

I am having a great trip—don't know where I am, but my master and my mom brought me here in a funny car on the water that they push with sticks. There are some great smells here. I think I'll go for a swim. Arrow the Dog.
—INLET FLOW

However, bringing man's best friend isn't always a good idea.

I've got my dog out for her first backpacking trip. No need to hang my food! Almost hung the stupid dog. First she rolls in shit at the parking lot, then her pack breaks as she is leaping across a brook, then she hassles the only other person for miles around, and then this soaking wet and stinky beast crashed out on my sleeping bag! She also wants to sleep in the fireplace. It just goes to show you that heaven for a dog is a bit different than for a person.
—DUCK HOLE 1

The presence of mice and chipmunks attracts their natural predators.

Stopped for lunch. The lake is a bit windy for canoeing. We saw a snake—black with yellow stripes that had just caught a frog and was in the process of swallowing it. A rare sight—or gruesome (from the frog's point of view). Anyway we watched it for a while—the snake was pretty much immobilized while it swallowed—so it was unable to crawl

In low light
Beneath low clouds,
A lone loon questioning
The echo of its call.

—CARRY

away. There was at least one other much smaller snake (possibly two) coiled with the big one (offspring?) One seemed to be perched on the back watching the drama unfold. The frog was still kicking a bit. Then there was blood around the snake's mouth and head. Overall a pretty gory site—but absolutely fascinating. Later we noticed a second larger snake farther away. So campers—be fore-warned. There are snakes about!!!
—*Janecks Landing*

The abundance of wildlife doesn't mean there aren't some identification problems. Mountain lions (or panthers, or wildcats) are generally believed to have been extirpated from the Adirondacks years ago, although there are still occasional sightings of unknown reliability. The following was one of the more questionable ones.

During the night we heard what we thought was a pair of owls but soon learned that it was a pair of mountain lions. They came to the edge of the clearing behind the tents and howled for a few minutes before moving on.
—STREETER LAKE

What they probably heard were coyotes, wild dogs, or their hybrid, coy-dogs, the topic of which is an ongoing debate at diner counters throughout the Adirondacks. This debate has spilled over to the registers.

We went in search of firewood. As I reached the junction of the lean-to & the main trails, I startled a coyote that was defecating at the junction. Only it was kind of lying down. It staggered to its feet, walked a few steps, and then just turned and watched. Tom came up the path and he/she moved a little farther down the trail, just stopped and turned its head to watch us. Tom walked toward it to scare it off (concerned it's sick & might come around the lean-to

tonight), and we heard another coyote howl in the distance. What's the connection between the two, does the other know how sick this one is? He/she waddled off—sick or dying.
—STEPHENS POND

A few entries later:

Regarding the sick coyote … we smelled the odor of a dead animal near the spring just south of the junction of the lean-to trail and the main trail. We found a "coy-dog" dead just up the hill from the trail. Coy-dogs are smaller than coyotes. They are part coyote and part domestic (gone wild) dog. Their nose is shorter than a coyotes. The ears are also shorter. A coy-dog may have brown fur, while a coyote's is usually gray. Coy-dogs may be the same size or larger than a coyote. They usually are less afraid of people than coyotes. Those who have the nose for it can see a dead coy-dog not far from the trail.
—STEPHENS POND

Penciled next to this entry: *This guy doesn't have a clue as to what he's talking about.*

Here is an unusual occurrence. Note that the kind of attacks reported here were mentioned by others throughout the register.

All three of us got attacked separately by two falcons in the woods on our way from Catlin Bay. A falcon actually hit me in the head and left claw marks on my hat, no joke.
—COLD RIVER 4

A lot of us go to the woods to have the experience of being close to nature in a setting where wild animals have had little contact with, and so are relatively unafraid of, humans.

The last pair of entries capture some of these moments.

As we sat on the rocks in front of this lean-to we were fortunate enough to witness a fawn swimming toward us from the opposite side of the pond. Pushing through the lily pads it came within a few yards as we all sat motionless—so close that we could hear its heavy breathing. Then it veered to the right as it became aware of our presence, presumably to get to the shore further out of site.
—STONY POND

Late last night around 11:00 or so we had a medium-sized fire roaring. Luckily we each had a stump to sit on as we chatted about the trip and other small talk. I was the first to hear something walking in the woods. From experience I knew it was not a tiny chipmunk, nor did it have the weight of a bear. I told my boyfriend and we both listened to the sound that was getting closer. Eventually my boyfriend shined his flashlight toward the sound, I think he would agree that we were equally anxious and excited about what we would see. Finally the light hit the animal form and we found it to be a doe, all alone, hunting for food. This being nothing unusual to see in the woods, we got back to the warmth of the fire.

As we talked a bit more we noticed the doe had moved closer to our campsite. In fact she was so close we no longer needed a flashlight to see her. This surprised us because all the deer we have seen in the woods has always been moving away from us, quite frightened by humans.

When she was about 10 feet away and staring intently at the fire I began speaking softly and kindly to her hoping to make her feel comfortable. Within about 10 minutes she was standing opposite of where were seated in front of the fire! She was actually drawn to the fire. We were flabbergasted, yet we remained very calm and quiet soaking in this beautiful experience.

Minutes passed and I decided to go to her to see if she would allow me to. She did. I was actually standing next to this creature and stroking her coarse fur on her back. She stayed and eventually my boyfriend stood up and did the same!

After about five minutes she calmly went back into the woods searching for food.

I have gotten a lot out of this experience. It has been the only thing I could think about all day. As humans we must realize how very little we know about animals. We must realize how intelligent they really are. How they feel love, safety, comfort as well as fear, hate, and pain. They feel and think just as humans do but in a different way.

—Klondike

Loons and beaver on lake in the cold A.M.
The coyotes howled at the full moon all night
And the grouse drummed a melody.

—Stephens Pond

On Behalf of all the deer flies on Chub Pond we would like to thank you for your swatting and cursing. One of our maney groups of escort flies will be leading you back to the safety of your car. Try not to knock yourself out when whacking at us. (It just makes us angry

Loyal order of DEER Flies
Local #27
Honorable Anne Noying

Anne Noying

P.S.
It's only 5.2 miles to safety.
Dont worry we will get you there!

8-21-01

12

Bugs

We gave blood at the Cascade Lake Lean-to.
—CASCADE POND

HANDLERS FOR HILARY CLINTON'S senate campaign are said to have dismissed the Adirondacks as a vacation destination because "there's nothing there but blackflies." Perhaps presuming this a slur on the region's overwhelmingly Republican majority, Hilary's next visit to the region (well, the outskirts of the region, since there are relatively few wealthy Democrat donors actually within the Blue Line) was met by a swarm of Adirondackers dressed in blackfly suits. No word on how the mosquitoes and deerflies felt about being left out.

The density and near suicidal hunger of the region's insect life has been remarked upon (to put it as politely as possible) in the journal of almost everyone visiting the Adirondacks. This 1869 account from "Wachusett," a scribe for the *Boston Daily Advertiser*, is a classic example.

I have seen parties hurrying back to the haunts of men from camps which they had sought but a few days before with high hopes of pleasure, driven away solely and simply by the stings of these little torments. I have heard of a gentleman, a sportsman, a journalist, the representative of a sporting paper, who came into the woods for a long stay, bringing four hundred pounds of baggage, and who discharged his guide after five days and sped back to the city ... I have seen a gentleman so disfigured by mosquitoes that he sought a resting place where his bites might heal before he would present himself to his friends. I have known those temporarily deprived of sight and hearing by mosquito bites ...

This account was obviously retouched in the insect-free environment of the scribe's parlor. In the field, the average bug-related entry is extremely short; the author simply cannot free his or her hand from swatting long enough to write more than a word or two.

Reading a series of bug-related entries in succession can result in that crawling feeling that accompanies the first few moments viewing a particularly seedy looking hotel room mattress. Often you simply realize you are screwed, and leave: *Bugs, Bugs, Bugs—in and out. Cage Lake Springhole.*

At the height of the bug season, there is a sort of desperate quality to the entries. You shake your head and sigh, "Poor bastards." *The bugs are closing in. I don't have much time ... Big Shallow.*

At their worst, there is no escape.

Bugs, bugs, bugs. Nothing but bugs. Bug spray doesn't help. Citronella candles won't help. Even Benadryl doesn't help! Humongous deerflies, menacing mosquitoes, and the most no-see-ums I've ever seen.
—HIGH FALLS EAST

[The author above] is my sister. The bugs just don't give up. I must have killed a thousand flies already. I wonder if in the future bugs will rule the world?
—HIGH FALLS EAST

Note: In the Adirondacks, they already do!

Bug season in the Adirondacks can be divided into four overlapping phases. As spring begins and the air warms, the first mosquitoes venture forth. These advance elements are usually small and slow; they are merely scouting for the real scourge of the woods: *Blackflies!*

Don't you people have anything better to worry about then the bears? Personally I fear the black flies more. The odds of being eaten by flies or black bears lean heavily toward the insects.
—GRIFFIN RAPIDS

Small, fast, prone to swarm, and not always detectable when feasting, they leave a bite that itches persistently, until its owner scratches it bloody, which then replaces the itch with genuine pain and, sometimes, infection. Small children have been hospitalized by particularly ferocious attacks.

As blackfly season waxes, part one of mosquito season begins in earnest. Early season mosquitoes tend to swarm, substituting with numbers what any individual lacks in speed or agility. Swatting one side of the neck simply leaves an opening on the other side, not to mention the unguarded hand.

Hudson Valley C.C. students lost 4 pints of blood in twelve hours to the mosquitoes. Severe anemia amongst crew. Signed, Crew EMT.
—GRIFFIN RAPIDS

Just as the blackflies and mosquitoes begin to thin out with the hotter weather of June, out come the deer flies! Buzzing in persistent circles around your head, their specialty is the kamikaze dive onto your scalp; you'd better squoosh them in your hair before they leave you with a painful bite. *Nice day but kind of cloudy. Deer flies as big as cats, no fish. Burntbridge Pond.*

Then, after a brief lull, comes part two of mosquito season. Second season mosquitoes favor dark and moist places. See that beautiful fern glen beside the trail? Keep walking—it's an ambush! These mosquitoes are crafty; slowly, slowly they circle, waiting for an opening. They are often nocturnal, rendering the sheltering concept of the lean-to irrelevant; you will never again forget your tent after a night spent with these annoying creatures.

What I love about the Adirondacks is the non-unionized mosquito population. In Alaska the mosquitoes swarm together or not at all. Here they work alone, eschewing the wolf pack tactics of their brethren. Like kamikazes of a dying mosquito empire they make their final fatal run through the searching headlamps … only to be met by the steely hand of fate! God bless DEET. It'll give you neurological deficits, but its worth it!
—COLD RIVER 3

Throughout the summer there is the steady drone of midges, no-see-ums, punkies, and other assorted flying things, a low- to medium-level chorus of irritation, annoyance, and itching.

Remedies for the assorted bites of the woodland-dwelling insect world abound, ranging from a skin product sold by the Avon Company to Vietnam-era chemical concoctions that began life as jungle defoliants. At full strength, the latter leave a peculiar burning sensation in the sensitive regions of the body, resulting in that uneasy "this can't be good for me" feeling associated with funny noises in jetliners and unplanned tours of time-share resorts.

My grandfather disposed of his cigarette butts in a coffee tin of water. He bottled the fragrant brown liquid and applied it to his forearms without dilution on our summer panfishing trips. When I was older I realized that the reason he didn't smoke in our tiny jon boat wasn't to spare me his evil habit in such close quarters; rather, he had inadvertently discovered the nicotine patch! No wonder his worms always seemed instantly paralyzed, and that even at a young age I caught more fish.

Insect Repellent: Ole Time Woodsmen. Liquid Fly Dope, pine scented. Mixed with 1 part Deep Woods Off, 1 part Cutter, 2 parts Skin So Soft, ice. Shake first 4 items, pour over ice and enjoy.
—PHARAOH

The tried-and-true remedy:

The bugs are extremely bad but built a smudge fire and it helped. Just got here and caught 2 nice trout and they are emerging all over the place. Only one cure for the bugs. LOTS OF BOOZE!!
—CAGE LAKE SPRINGHOLE

As well as the homemade:

Mosquitoes are bad and also the black flies so I decided to make a flyswatter with paper, stick and two rubber bands.
—BURNTBRIDGE POND

Don't count on any of it working.

The deer flies are outrageous. They are bighting us to death so we are leaving today … don't even bother using DEET for these things, its a waste of time.
—CAGE LAKE SPRINGHOLE

A common novice mistake, and one certainly never repeated:

To women who are hiking: I made the mistake of washing my hair this morning with strawberry essence shampoo. I've become the landing field for all the flies on this path!
—STEPHENS POND

Nearly every register is festooned with the smeared bodies of former members of the insect world. These are often accompanied with inscriptions, introducing us to the deceased and describing the circumstances of his or her demise. Many appear to have at least enjoyed a last meal before finding eternity in a very flat place.

There is nothing quite like the release of finally getting inside a building or car and away from the vicious hordes plaguing a particularly buggy trip. One effective survival strategy is to bring along bait.

Beginners trek of Adirondack Canoe Expedition run out of St. Regis. Was up at High Falls yesterday & loved the noise & lack of bugs. Going back to Inlet tomorrow &

giving the bug-chewed kids back to their parents. Praying that no lawsuits ensue.
—GRIFFIN RAPIDS

No doubt the kids were issued the wholly worthless "children's formula" repellent while the counselors kept the high-octane stuff for themselves.

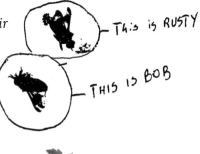

THIS is RUSTY

THIS IS BOB

13

Grub

Butter, cinnamon, brown sugar, apples, foil. Slice apples in half, scoop out core/seeds. Fill w/ butter, sugar and cinnamon. Wrap in foil and place in coals till soft to touch.
—CASCADE POND

I USED TO GO WINTER CAMPING in the Blue Ridge with my high school buddies, one of whom consistently astonished us with his culinary skills. There we'd be, hopping up and down, thumping our arms across our chests with no other thought than to stay warm. Daniel, who had an array of stove-mounted cookware not duplicated in any single catalog, would meanwhile be whipping up a bundt cake on a single burner Svea. I always made sure Daniel was going before I'd agree to a winter trip.

I've always been more of a Vienna Sausage-and-beans kind of camper, frankly grateful to mooch anything that looked better, which is to say, almost everything. Not everybody is as sensible.

7 pm raining again. The mutinous hounds are now salivating over McDonalds Big Macs. After preparing yet another culinary feast for them, the camp cook is stewing under his hat. Ingrates! They feast upon the finest mutton in the Five Ponds–Oswegatchie area, yet are not satisfied.
—CAGE LAKE SPRINGHOLE

As is widely known, there are those who live to eat, and those who eat to live. As with any relationship, culinary happiness on a camping trip depends on compromise and accommodation. (Alternately, the secret may be to "strategically ignore each other," as one of my married buddies advised during my bachelor party, but somehow I think this thought should remain firmly attached to the marital, rather than the camping, realm).

Subject: World's best burrito cooking places.
Background: Sue is the adventurous type. Paul likes to cook and eat. Sue thinks this is OK too.
Problem: Sue needs hiking/camping partners.
Solution: Paul will go only if he can have a leisurely hot lunch along the way.
Adventure: After our 4th hike together stopping at every lunch hour to make hot burritos, we have found the peak of Noonmark to be the superior burrito joint so far. This is undoubtedly indispensable information to the gourmet backpacker.
Tomorrow's Dilemma: Sue wants to go on to climb Dix. Paul wants to chill at the lean-to & chow on blueberry muffins and hot toddies. Perhaps Sue's surprise snacks of homemade brownies and swiss chocolate will spur Paul into action and achieve new culinary heights on top of Mt. Dix. Perhaps not—tune in tomorrow.
—BOQUET RIVER

Cooks are generally wonderful people, especially when they share their special secrets.

Cooking Tip: Boil spaghetti water Add spaghetti—let boil till soft—strain water off through crack in lid—dump spaghetti on ground—rinse—serve.
—GRIFFIN RAPIDS

Cooking Tip #2—Grilled Eggplant: Slice eggplant & put in enclosed cooking rack. Keep turning until eggplant is golden brown. Pick up rack over fire and spill contents into fire (accompanying the act with lots of swearing), retrieve eggplant (and ash) and put back in rack. Cook 10 more minutes to burn off the ash. When ready lift rack off fire & open rack upside down dumping eggplant on the ground. More swearing and jumping up & down. Pick up eggplant and throw in fire.
—GRIFFIN RAPIDS

Recipes too.

Iroquois lean-to in fair shape for age. Although being next to stream does attract a great number of snakes. Speaking of snakes, here's a great recipe for your next trail dinner:

Start w/ 4 snakes (any variety), 2 frogs (mature), 3 dozen black flies, and a finger of your hiking companion. Remove heads from snake, frog, and flies (not companion) and set in 3/4 c. boiling water for stock. Bring to boil and let simmer for 15 min. While stock is simmering sauté frog and snake remains in own juices for 1 min. then pan blacken with carbon from bottom of cooking vessel. Add flour to stock, thicken, pour onto snake/frog. Garnish with finger.
—WALLFACE

Allow me to pass on to you my recipe for black fly soup.

1. Pour two cups of water into bowl.
2. Allow to sit uncovered for approximately one minute (time necessary for a swarm of flies to hover over pot may vary).
3. Clamp lid briskly and firmly over top.
4. Bring to boil. Add extra minute for revenge.
5. Enjoy!
—DUCK HOLE 1

Gorp Recipe

2 cups peanuts
1 cup M&Ms
1 cup raisins
¹/₄ tsp mouse turds
Combine in plastic bag. Toss lightly. Serve at room temper-
ature. Or leave your homemade gorp on the lean-to floor
and you will have the same thing.
—DUCK HOLE 1

Some people really know what they're doing.

We're three hikers from various places who stumbled upon
one of the forest's greatest gifts: "Boleats," a kind of mush-
room found at this time of year. We sliced it up, and sliced
it looked like bacon. We sautéed it in butter (tastes like
nothing else, just fabulous flavor, an exceptional taste.
Earthy, nutty and meaty, reminded Chris of catfish). Later
on in our meal we had Morel French Onion Soup that will
leave an indelible impression on this lean-to.
—ROCKY FALLS

Well-cooked food in the outdoors after a long day on the
trail is truly one of the best things about camping. However,
after a long day on the trail, almost anything will do.

You know what the best thing about camping is? Most peo-
ple get all mushy and talk about "bonding with the trees"
and "enjoying the zen-like serenity," but that stuff is all
bogus … the best thing about camping is you get to eat all
sorts of nifty junk food that you would never be eating oth-
erwise! When I'm at home I eat brown rice and tofu and
birdseed and other healthy stuff, but when I'm camping,
bring on the Franco-American! We've got pop-tarts, canned
mac and cheese, canned hash, baked beans, etc. But its all

A day in the Oswi,
With all going well.
We pulled into 38
With all looking swell.

We put on some dinner
To keep us all going.
But the noodles and cheese
Left us all knowing
That this stuff was awful
It stinks, it was gross!
We just couldn't do it
Not even one dose!

While dying of hunger
Was not in the offing,
We were all growing
Weak and were coughing.

When just at our darkest
There came out of the mist,
The Good Humor Man
With a very long list.
Of ice cream and sodas
And twinkie like goodies, and
Pies, and candy, and
Other sweet tasting stuff.

We all had our fill,
Enjoying each bite,
And before you could wink,
He had paddled out of sight.

—GRIFFIN RAPIDS

ok because we're camping! In fact, I once went on a camping trip where we ate nothing but crunch 'n munch, jiffy pop, turtle wax and Budweiser for 11 days! Admit it: you're all just here for the junk food. I may even convert this lean-to into a Domino's pizza franchise.

—SILVER LAKE

14

The Privy

Welcome to Griffin Rapids Latrine. Whosoever passeth in, shall surely passeth out.
—GRIFFIN RAPIDS

T HE PRIVY HOLDS AN ICONIC POWER, evoking horror even among those for whom wearing a week's worth of dirt is a badge of honor. I'm certain that the prospect of having to use the privy keeps a significant number of people from going camping, and I've had several companions who somehow shut down all bowel functions for the duration of a trip rather than face the horrors within.

By the way—if you have to use the outhouse in the middle of the night, try not to. Every Friday the 13th movie will be racing through your head. Remember the one where a person was stabbed in the outhouse—right through the wall? Anyway, just a thought.
—STONY POND

Privies are usually sited and constructed by the DEC, often with the assistance of ADK volunteers. Every few years they become full and a new one must be dug. Occasionally they are outfitted with improvements.

Nice lean-to and the privy has a rainbow air freshener. Now just need a plug for my cappuccino maker.
—STEPHENS POND

On an extended backpacking trip long ago, my friend and I invented a fairly involved rating system for outhouses and the contents therein. Points were awarded for cleanliness, quality of tissue (if any), presence of reading material, etc. Turns out this backwoods amusement was not unique to us.

Just passin' thru on the last few miles of an end to ender. The "Latrine Committee" of the end-to-enders vote the Moose Lake lean-to latrine the most pleasant and hygienic. Congratulations! Your prize is a large carton of Charmin toilet paper. It may be claimed in Lake Placid.
—MOOSE POND

The sheer terror of the privy causes some to lug in their own personal latrines, sometimes with unfortunate results. Although stinky, Adirondack outhouses are at least professionally constructed. This entry is from a lean-to some eight miles from the trailhead.

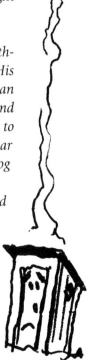

Last night was the funniest night I've ever spent. My brother-in-law had brought along a port-a-potty just in case. His two sons had each used it before we found out there was an outhouse. Well old Dad wakes up about 2:00 a.m. and nature's callin'. A little skittish about bears, he decides to use his little port-a-potty. Well, while he's sitting on bear watch doing some business suddenly out of nowhere a frog jumps on his foot!

Things got a little messy at this point. The john collapsed and my brother-in-law did a seat-drop into the unthinkable. I just heard the collapse and a few choice words and that was it, the whole camp was in an uproar.

We all apologized for laughing about an hour after it happened and this morning he can find a "little" humor in it. Needless to say we made him take a bath before coming back to bed.
—CAGE LAKE SPRINGHOLE

The subject of outhouses leads us naturally to other bodily functions. Backpacking rations, especially the freeze-dried variety, have a deserved reputation for inducing flatulence. One of the advantages of the lean-to in this regard is the excellent ventilation it provides. A friend and I once nearly asphyxiated in a two-man tent that could not be unzippered because of a driving rainstorm. The culprit was my dog, who never again partook of the brand of dog food bought to replace that which I had forgotten. This particular problem isn't always bad news though.

Skied in. G. very flatulent from New Years celebrations. I skied behind and he kept me warm. Chilly day otherwise.
—STONY POND

Like dogs, men often mark their territory. This habit is best observed on a canoe trip; see if the need does not arise at every stop, no matter how frequent they may be.

We are visiting Cedar Point from Beaver Point (which should be renamed Piss Point or Bladder Control Problem Point or the Point of Yellow Snow or something).
—CEDAR POINT

Bathroom walls are frequently adorned with poetry, much of it scatological or worse. This practice is rarely found in the Adirondack privy, presumably because of the difficulty involved both in writing on the wooden walls and in maintaining residence long enough to complete the creative act. In consequence, those moved to create verse use the registers. We conclude with two examples.

ODE TO THE OUTHOUSE

Oh Outhouse
You do not contain a louse
And Upon Thee I do sit
To make my daily shit.
Oh, thou art very clean
A joy to have seen.

Thy walls are brown & tan
To use you I just ran
My mother & my sister
Say it's just a joy to have you, mister
And my father
Says you're rather
Just a joy to the beholder.

—Ouluska Pass

Ten girls in tents
We're lucky gents.
Such happy smiling faces
To share these wonderful places.
And now they're gone
We'll hear no more
The slamming of the outhouse door!

—Wolf Jaw

15

The Campfire

We came, we sawed and we had a nice fire.
—HAMILTON STREAM

FOR MANY, THE FIRE SYMBOLIZES the camping experience. The scent and crackle, the hypnotic flames, the stories, the laughter. When I was growing up, my friends and I competed to see who could build the best campfire. The goal, to start it with a single match, was achieved by the perfect arrangement of kindling, twigs, and sticks. How things change; now, on family outings to the local state park, I am not above employing lighter fluid.

We entered on the Falls Pond Trail and were immediately welcomed to this pristine forest by a choice selection of beaver walking sticks. The day was long. The air was thick with anticipation of a weekend communing with the native flora of this wilderness. After an evening of competition we settled around the fire, the fire being that of a choice aged birch log, of approximately 4" diameter, cut into precisely 13" logettes, split with fervor and ardor, by Sylvio Jr., with a knife of unusual mass, and constructed in the style of the Adirondack "box fire." The fire, constructed so, provided us with the necessary warmth and security that fires, although not of such construction, have provided many men for thousands of years. And as manly men often do, we discussed the details of the days frog hunt, often in colorful dance and mime.
—WEST CANADA LAKE

At one time, all lean-tos were equipped with fireplaces of some sort (and most still are). They are usually built of local fieldstone and generally have convenient metal grates that can be lifted for unrestricted access and raised or lowered for optimum pot placement. Occasionally they are built against large, flat boulders, with results both aesthetically pleasing and heat radiating, as at Brooktrout Lake: *We were so pleased to have brought our slide projector when we saw the fireplace.*

*Campfire light lights up
The inside of lean-to and
The underside of pine boughs
Campfire light—good as
Jingle Bells at makin' spirits
Bright—campin' out tonight.*

—WOLF LAKE

Over time lean-tos acquire a motley assortment of outdoor cooking supplies hung by passing campers on nails within and without: pots and pans, narrow-gauge grills, wiener forks, tongs, spatulas, matches, tin foil. Cleaning supplies such as sponges and towels rarely survive the resident mice for more than a night or two, unless carefully bagged. Other things accumulate.

And then we pondered … all night we pondered … even in the rain we pondered—why the plastic hose section?
—COLD RIVER 1

Just because it's protected from the elements on three sides doesn't mean fire starting is easy. For one thing, dry wood is a necessity, and it's not sold at a nearby camp store. Adirondack tradition holds that a quantity of wood equal to that which was used should be placed within or under the lean-to so that it dries for the next camper. Like many traditions, this one appears to have waned in recent years. The registers report many tales of the difficulties faced by those trying to start fires with wet wood.

Tried to light a fire last night with rain-soaked wood and damp tinder. After 30 min. of dizzying head rushes, trying to blow life into wet wood, we left it for dead, and sat to eat

our grilled bear for dinner. (Pete caught and killed it with his "bear" hands—hee hee—on the way up Yard yesterday.) Actually it was Lipton's Stroganoff—a tasty treat ... Much to our surprise, after 5 bites of goo, and with us no closer than 10 feet to the failed fire, flames danced to life on the logs! Whooowhee!! Pete dried his crusty Bucknell hat, and we sat in silence for an hour, entranced by the fire. Nothing could touch or hurt us ... All there was was the fire, the brook, the fading light, and then the night; it was still, and quiet, and we slept. Amen.
—KLONDIKE

Often, the registers are the only source of material with which to ignite a fire; a significant percentage of registers are thus never completed and meet a combusted destiny (thus fulfilling, it can be argued, one of their backcountry life-support functions). It is a rare register that is not missing at least a few pages.

Hike was lovely, weather cold as a butt, and ice everywhere, so cold that it was hard to start the fire, so we used the rest of the paper in this book! I would tell you our names but you might get mad at us for the paper and come to get us.
–HAMILTON STREAM

Various admonitions followed the entry above, but it's hard

to argue with the need on a bitterly cold or wet day. Once started, the campfire serves many functions besides cooking and warmth; for example, drying wet boots, socks, and clothes—often with predictable results. *My mother burned my shoes in the fire* is an entry found in nearly every register.

Responsible outdoorspeople have for many years cooked on backpacking stoves, rather than on a campfire, because of the destruction caused by the demand for firewood. Although it is illegal to cut standing timber in the Adirondack Forest Preserve, the practice is common at popular campsites where often not a single stick can be scavenged from the ground for hundreds of yards surrounding.

I have a suggestion for the people sawing on the live trees. GO BACK WHERE YOU CAME FROM AND LEAVE THESE WOODS ALONE! Some folk's don't have the sense God gave a carrot.
—WANIKA FALLS

The realization that campfires have adverse impacts has grown over time. But there is an even more basic disagreement, and that is the need for the fire itself. Just as the fire hypnotizes, it also cuts you off from the night and what is going on around you.

On the "other" side of the trail I noticed quite a few green trees knocked, cut or sawn over, evidently as future supplies of fires. The ultimate solution to this is to ban fires completely, and I'd be for that if this vandalism continues. Seriously, try camping without a fire—it's not as cold, desperate or lonely as it sounds. A fire isolates you and yours from the night, from the loons, from the wilderness, from the very things you are out here for. Last night I had my first fire in over 50 nights of camping—I was alone and it

was cold and felt like I needed it—but rarely do I miss having a fire. If you need a "flame fix" to act as a focus for your evenings conversation, try a candle(s).
—SOUTH LAKE

In 2000 the DEC instituted a ban on campfires in the eastern High Peaks because of the damage being done to the forest. Judging from the registers, this move has been very unpopular. This entry is from an individual styling himself the Forest Warrior Society. He or she has left numerous entries in many log books over the years complaining about all sorts of perceived environmental mismanagement being practiced by the DEC, including, oddly enough, the fire policy.

Calling all jumba-wumba tub thumpers/budding Black Panthers/jungle dancers—gonna' mount an offensive against the State's latest heavy handed, repressive wilderness management practices—talkin' newly instituted bans on the time honored traditions of campfires and back country camping in the High Peaks. Whatever happened to site specific fire restrictions? Don't you get it NYSDEC? You don't have to kill the wilderness experience to save the High Peaks. Calling all wilderness visitors—calling for enmasses non-violent civil disobedience.
—KAGEL

I'm the cookout campfire.
I sizzle and snap
As I burn down to coals
To roast a hot dog
For Amazin' Annie

I'm the campfire.
I crackle and blaze
As I burn down to coals
To roast three hot dogs
for Cave Man Dave

I'm the campfire.
That burned for but an hour
On the 30th of May 93
On the granite slab out in
Front of the lean-to in the
Wild rocky shores of Wolf Lake.

—WOLF LAKE

16

A Long Walk Here

Four overweight slobs dragged our butts through the snow from Rt. 73. Not used to 60 lbs. of pack.
—BOQUET RIVER

I GREW UP A DISCIPLE of Colin Fletcher's *The Complete Walker.* Although containing some valuable tips, I'm afraid it encouraged an unfortunate sense of regimentation in my personal hiking style: exactly fifty minutes of marching, followed by a precise ten-minute rest. Repeat until blistered. Consult foot care chapter. (I blame Fletcher's Special Forces background for imposing this style, and my German heritage for adopting it.) At any rate, it did not make me the most pleasant of hiking companions, except perhaps to my Appalachian Trail hiking buddy with whom I attempted to keep pace for a few weeks one summer long ago.

Because the business of AT through hiking is generally conducted solo, with partners meeting at the end of each day for that special bonding that occurs among the truly miserable, it really didn't matter at all to John how I managed to drag my exhausted ass to the shelter each evening. All that mattered to him was that I had successfully lugged the necessary half of our communal food supplies so that he could consume four thousand or so calories and then collapse into his nightly coma.

Exhaustion is perhaps the most common result of a full day of backpacking.

I'm Jessica and my soulmate Mike & I are hiking the NP Trail. Today is our 6th day. We got a ride from a wonderful man w/a big truck. That cuts today's mileage to about 7 miles! I am so relieved. We're from near Albany. I need to rest now.
—STEPHENS POND

Too tired to write! Poor Jessica! Poor Mike! I wonder if their soul mating survived the trip?

Anyway, for me this phase lasted longer than was sensible. Though in those days I thought of myself as an all-around major hiking dude, I now know that I wasn't fit to mix some of these people's gorp.

Arrived here about 4:00 & am tired (35 miles since 3:30 yesterday afternoon). Am running (and walking) the trails for 9 days—hope to average 18–20 miles/day. Have all my backpack gear including 2 days food +1.5 pt water down to 15 lb in day pack and fanny pack. Start at Lake Durant and will go to Placid then Keene Valley via JB Lodge then to Duck Hole and Lake Durant (out) … Mosquitoes bad but 100% DEET does the trick. Was attacked by a mad mother grouse yesterday.
—OULUSKA PASS

The grouse was probably pissed at getting caught in a shower of bug repellant as he jogged by.

At some point I came to the great realization that maybe the idea wasn't to be quite so achievement oriented, but simply to be in, and enjoy being in, The Woods. I'd like to believe my epiphany came from listening to one too many competitive campfire conversations in which the participants strove to outdo one another with tales of peaks summited and bushes whacked, but I suspect it may have more to do with advancing age and its associated maturity, to mention nothing of the incredible pain in my knees when I backpack more than ten miles a day. Still, I choose to blame guys like this.

In the Lean-to
A breeze comes up
And says "Hello"
To me, then passes on
Like a traveler
Enjoys the
Stories created
In a journey.
Everything is
Here if you look close:
The fire burning
A month ago
Camp food burnt
And undercooked
Tasting scrumptious
Because of all
Today's steps
That create
The appetite.

KLONDIKE

The weather certainly has been cooperative so far on this year's phase of "Adirondack Adventures." "Base Camp" here tonight prior to a bushwhack of the 2 main peaks of Blue Ridge just a few miles SW of here. Hiking the Adirondacks Hundred Highest. Of course, depending on whose list you use, you may hike different peaks. So we are using 2 "100 highest lists." Fortunately most of the peaks on one list are included on the other, but the total is going to be more like 115.

Thus far we've done I think 74, of which 73 are in the list in the ADK High Peaks Guide Book. So tomorrow we'll make 76 (75), barring unforeseen emergencies, and hopefully return here the same day (??) Gonna carry the full packs up there anyhow, just in case, ya know.

Well, we hope to get all "100" peaks bagged before we leave in about a month. If not maybe we'll be back in the fall, maybe not until next year. Oh yeah, the "5-year plan" includes chipping away at the two hundred some odd "ADK 3,000-footers."

Any other really serious peak baggers out there please write. I'd like to trade notes, stories and the like. Heck, I'd just like to know that I'm not the only nut in the woods doing this sort of thing. "46-ers" are not necessarily the sort I'm looking for, but if you plan to go on to smaller and

(maybe) better things, please drop a line. ADK 46er, NE 111er, NH 4,000'ers, New England 4,000'ers, New England Hundred Highest, S.E. Beyond 6,000 (plan to do Catskill 3500 this winter), A.T. Ga-Me ('84 & '87), NPT ('86), Vt. Long Trail, Va/WV Big Blue Trail, Pa./Md Tuscarora trail, Wva/Va Allegheny trail, Pa Loyalsock Trail & many others.
—STEPHENS POND

Nevertheless, achievement occasionally beckons. Psychologists tell us our personalities are hard-wired so that whatever we are at age two is what we'll always be. (Sorry, bed-wetters!) I can see myself in my dotage staggering up the muddy path to "Nubbletip" some early December day (having misread the calendar), like this poor fellow.

Going for Hough over Dix tomorrow for a new world's record of every mountain or terrain that has a name over 4000 feet east of the Mississippi in Continental USA. All within 2½ years. Have made two attempts at Hough from Dix South on the bail out herd trail and both have failed. Hoping to bushwhack the ridgeline south from Dix thru Col and back up Hough then return to lean-to. Wish me luck as I am getting real tired.
—LILLIAN BROOK

A note in his hand follows saying he made it, only to have his achievement greeted thus in the next entry.

It's kind of odd that the first thing he said to us was "I just broke the God-damned world record!" The old geaser looked a little out of place, half naked, his body sagging under a gortex parka. "Every peak over 4000 east of the Mississippi, under 2½ years." We gaped in awe at the seemingly miraculous feat of this aging He-Man. "My 3rd attempt at Hough (pronouncing it "Hoag") This comment snapped me out of my trance of admiration as I pondered how anyone could piece together a 3 day assault on Hough. Detecting an attentive audience he produced a small piece of paper from his pocket. "You've heard of McMartin haven't you?" Wondering if this was some sort of trick question I said "no" and began to wait for his response. He turned around and began fumbling through a frame pack. "Well this girl McMartin, she's about 60 now but in her picture she looks about 30, well she puts out a herd trail map." We huddled around him as he displayed the map and paper. "This'll tell you how to get from Dix to Hough. I blazed my own trail from the beckhorn (pronounced belk-corn) to Hough." (still pronounced Hoag). My friend gave me a messed up look of amazement and confusion, wondering if this old man of the mountains refuses to use obvious herd paths.

"Did you find a herd path?" I probed. "Well, if you want to take my route you can't miss it with the blazes." My god, I thought, this old man forces his way through the cripple brush, completely oblivious to any herd paths. "As you can see I have a quadruple bypass" pointing out a scar on his chest. "I have to hyperventilate on the steep sections, or else I don't get enough oxygen to my lungs." He kneeled down and began rolling up his Therma-Rest in a dignified and methodical silence, the gray mop of hair bobbing up and down in a rhythmic fashion.

I couldn't bear it any longer. I found my way behind the lean-to where I could let out the mountain of silent laughter that had built up over the past 15 minutes. I tried so hard to retain it, it felt like dry-heaving. By the time I could muster up the courage to return to the front of the lean-to, he seemed ready to leave. As he left, my friends and I let out our accumulated laughter, but were still amazed at his feats. The next day we diligently removed every piece of fluorescent surveyor's tape he had left on the trees. The

Flaming Asshole had blazed the god damned herd path!!
—LILLIAN BROOK

This section includes trips made difficult by unusual events. We'll conclude with two accounts of travel in the High Peaks in the wake of Hurricane Floyd in September 1999.

I read the warning and saw the tape closing the trail to Macomb and the Dixes, but there was no such warning for the Elk Lake/Marcy Trail. It took me 9½ hours to hike 9 miles. I had to strip from the waste down to get over (through) the Ausable Inlet; the bridge is gone. I lost the trail and had to back track at least five times. Coming across Marcy Swamp was the worst. I had to leave the trail off the right side and bushwack for about ½ hour before I joined up with the trail again. I literally crawled on my belly in many spots.
—PANTHER GORGE

Now I lay me down to rest
A pile of maps upon my chest.
If I die before I wake
That's one less hike I have to take.

DUCK HOLE 1

I attempted to continue along the Dix Trail, but made only ¾ mile progress in two hours, injuring my left knee in the process. The trail is essentially impassable. Anyone contemplating going north should work upstream from here on what's left of the Macomb herd path for ½ mile, then turn north. Near the trail there are literally acres of downed trees, trunks piled 8'–12' high in places.
—SLIDE BROOK

If you hike these trails today, you will find them passable thanks to the work of ADK trail crews.

17

Adventures

We (12 of us) are with Gordon College taking a 12-day mountain adventure. We are on day one. And I think I can speak for all of us when I say, "MOOOOOMMMI-IEEE!!"
—*Blueberry*

WHAT'S A CAMPING TRIP without a few adventures? Quiet, peaceful, refreshing; sure. But for some, the backwoods experience means having an adventure. It might be climbing a big mountain (especially if it's trailless), or an extended trip into the wilderness. The longer and more remote the trip, the greater the likelihood of having an adventure.

The Seward Range comprises four trailless peaks over four thousand feet high and provides some of the most difficult hiking in the Adirondacks. If you want to be a Forty-Sixer, you need to conquer these mountains. *Warning: Unless you have serious sins to atone for, do not attempt to bushwhack the Sewards! Seward.* Those attempting the range must depart early in the morning and count on an approximately twelve-hour hike. It ain't easy.

Arose a bit late and left for Seward–Don–Emmons. Did not realize extent of the journey. We peaked Seward at 12:30 pm and proceeded to do the rest of the ridge. On Emmons we decided that a return trip over the ridge would be unwise, considering it took us six hours to get where we were, and it was already 4:30 pm. Elected to bushwhack down the SE side of Emmons. Very gnarly going. Eventually broke out onto a slide and caught the best view of the trip—All the High Peaks as clear as day—Unobstructed and divine.

Caught a stream at the bottom of the slide and followed it for more than an hour before we joined the Ouluska brook SE to Cold Brook (?) where we joined the Northville–Placid trail. Very tired and almost out of H_2O. It was almost dark and we had 9 miles to return. No flashlights.

Virtually ran to Rondeau's Hermitage and then stuck together due to darkness. Stars out and a lightning storm added to the freakish evening. Slowly, slowly returned to Blueberry via Horse trail—waded a bog that would be no trouble for a horse but was knee-deep for us. Lots of faith and a few spills saw us return at 2 am for dinner and deserved rest. Whew. Great trip!

—BLUEBERRY

The Adirondack Mountains are nowhere near as high as those in the American west, to say nothing of many other parts of the world, but mountains they are, and that means they offer the potential for severe weather in all seasons.

Came in from St. Huberts via Noonmark Mountain. It was drizzling and cool. Thought we had reached the peak four times before we found the real one. Visibility at the top was about 50 feet and a cold wet wind was howling across the

top. Took us 20 minutes in the wind before we finally found the trail. Gives new meaning to freezing your buns. We were ecstatic to find a clean, neat, uninhabited lean-to in which to spend the night.
—BOQUET RIVER

Came down from Phelps on the 14th. Climbed Algonquin in and out and back from here on the 15th. Nearly got blown off the mountaintop with 75–100 mph gusts. Had to crawl to the summit on hands and knees. Rained all last night. The ranger said, "The trail up Algonquin follows the river so it might be a little wet." What he should have said was, "The trail up Algonquin is the river so be prepared to get soaked."
—CEDAR POINT

Winter ascents come with their own unique challenges.

Set out with a daypack early Sunday morning (7:30 am— not early enough) for another attempt at Marshall. We are determined to make it this time. Breaking through 3' of snow on the trail up to Marshall is an arduous task. We get to what we think is a herd path at 11:30 am and start over the initial bump on our way to Marshall. Spirits are high and we feel good (temps in the mid 30's).

We never did get over that bump. The cripplebrush was thick and boy did it cripple us. The 3' of snow didn't help either. The path we were on was not a herd path but a path of our making. We got to 4160' in elev. where we ate lunch and decided to turn back. It was 2:00 pm by this time and we knew we would be fighting daylight.

A word of advice—if you plan to get Marshall in the winter, that you shouldn't attempt it from this lean-to, but as Keith once said "Better to have tried and failed then not to have tried at all." We packed

out early Monday morning bloodied but not beaten.
—ROCKY FALLS

Here's an account of a water-borne adventure from the Oswegatchie country.

Took our chances praying that the mighty Oswegatchie would crest and begin dropping before morning. The alternative of breaking camp in darkness and blindly heading downstream was not a real option. Well at 7:00 a.m., the river is still rising, bottom of lean-to submerged in 6" of water. Tents in back pine stand had to be evacuated at 4:00 a.m. as we sought out dry "knoll" just downstream of shelter. 39 degrees F and wind 10–12 mph, our feet are soaked but spirits good. We're packing up, emptied shelter using bucket brigade and canoes, our patch of dry land sinking fast.

What an escapade it's been! We've had it all. Warmth & sun, high winds making pines groan and campers nervous. Soaking rains all day yesterday. Scrambling through the massive blowdown. Now the memorable flood of '95. We shall return!
—CAGE LAKE SPRINGHOLE

The official purpose of the lean-tos is to serve as shelter for lost or injured hikers. The registers occasionally record "on-the-spot" accounts from injured hikers, as well as from those who encounter them.

Apparently will be sharing facilities with some youth, one of whom seems to have heat exhaustion. Group of eight whom we first met at Cold River 3 & 4 early today. They have one sick hiker. They were determined to get to Upper Works, but decided they'd have a better chance of quicker help if they went back to Long Lake where they might catch a ride from some boaters.
—OULUSKA PASS

Kevlar canoes—just 16 pounds
The perfect boat we thought we'd found
But then we met our greatest fear
What seemed like 70 pounds of gear.

The cool clear nights felt unseasonably like fall
And the long portages were quite the haul
And with overcast days inducing a slight malaise
We were saved by the meteor showers at which to gaze.

Serenaded by a lonely loon
Under the bright evening moon
We sympathized with his search for a mate
For it's been a time since we had a date.

One night we camped at a lovely little cove
All was well, till we tried to light the stove
It was a rather depressing sight
For it would nary light.

Things were looking rather dire
Till we started a roaring campfire
It was worth many a jewel
To warm our dehydrated gruel.

To make our daily evening grog
We had to cook over the burning log
So cleaning pots was rather a chore
The one part of the trip that was a bore.

The stove just needed a cleaning out
And dinner is no longer a 10-round bout
With the stove now a friend—not foe
We can more easily make a cup of joe.

We aimed for the campsite across the bay
But that plan was not to stay
A thunderstorm toward Fish Pond did roam
So we chose this lean-to as our home.

Four ponds left to paddle and three carries more
Tomorrow we'll both be a little sore
A long way out, a longer way in
But there are few places I'd rather have been.

—FISH POND 1

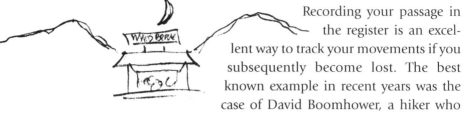

Recording your passage in the register is an excellent way to track your movements if you subsequently become lost. The best known example in recent years was the case of David Boomhower, a hiker who perished while through hiking the Northville–Placid Trail in 1990. He failed to record his decision in the Colden Brook Lean-to register to leave the main trail and take an obscure side route to Lewey Lake, where he hoped to resupply. He became disoriented on the little-used and poorly marked trail and decided to await rescue. It never came, because the searchers didn't know where to look; they were following the main trail where he had written he was continuing his hike.

Boomhower survived for more than two months before succumbing to starvation or exposure, while searchers scoured the trails along the route he had written he would be taking. As the weeks went by, his journal continually questioned why he hadn't been found. His body was eventually located by hunters.

Accounts of lost hikers are especially unnerving as you realize just how close some of these people are to life-threatening disaster. This entry is particularly worrisome because of the lack of basic safety procedures being followed with youth in the woods.

Ran into [boy] *at 4,000' on Phelps to Marcy at 3:55 trying to get to Marcy Dam. This 14 yr. old, by himself, observed coming down off Marcy with a youth group. We spent 20 mins approx 2:15 at trail junction. And no one was looking for him then and he was obviously lost from group and going down wrong trail. Sent him to JBL at 4 p.m., talked him out of climbing back up & then down as*

directed by someone at Slant Rock, kid had no flashlight and no experience. Would never have made it, especially before dark. When we got to Slant Rock they said the kid had gotten water and food from them. They also directed another lost boy to JBL (Scout troop based at JBL).
—BUSHNELL FALLS 3

One not as scary, but all too typical of the unprepared hiker.

Ended up in lean-to. We started our trek from Panther Gorge en route to Slant Rock. We had no map, no food, no water and it rained all day long … We ended up getting lost on our way here.

We were hiking from 8:00 a.m. to 7:00 p.m. We topped three mountains SE of here having no idea where we were. Wet, and one being injured (left knee) decided to backtrack eventually finding our way. The trails were very tough and all washed out with runoff.
—BUSHNELL FALLS 3

There are occasional near-misses.

A cold start after a hard night. Yesterday we skied in from the gate (4 hrs). Deep snow made slow going. Fairly light packs. Plans called for early a.m. start and a climb of the Dix Slide. We should have read the bad omens early on. First, Bill dropped his glove shell down the outhouse hole. Managed to use Chevinard poles as chopsticks to pluck it from the frozen mound. The temperature plummeted, hitting zero about 7 p.m.

Settling in, Bill managed to leak a water bottle in his sleeping bag. Crisis. We sopped most of the freezing water out, gave him extra parkas, pants, etc. and told him to stop whining. About 10 my water bottle (which I'd double checked and de-iced after Bill) leaked, waking me. 2nd

Crisis—wet rear, wet shoulder. I sopped and shivered, finally driving off enough moisture to sleep, fitfully. Naturally we missed our wake up call and decided to settle for a ski on Dix Pond. Learned a few things.
—LILLIAN BROOK

The bad-trips genre includes those who have been unable to complete their planned climb.

Failed to reach Seward Summit (started for truck trail 9:50 am). Got off herd path somehow; felt we'd gotten back on it; never really found terrain that seemed to match [the guidebook's] candid description (no "... ten foot headwall that will force you to the left ..."); decided to follow the brook. Tough scramble from there, almost all in the brook, straight up giant, wet boulders, but, surprisingly, no truly terrifying moments. We ended up at a point where we could possibly have bushwhacked up to the summit (500 ft below?) but by then it was 2:30 and we were in a cloud (no views). We (Dave and I) conferenced (briefly) and, in the end, late hour, bad view, and good sense sent us back down. We got a bit side tracked again coming down but really only long enough to eat a sandwich, decide to follow the feeder we were near, and have a smoke.

Came out feeling a little despondent but, all in all, we got 1 magnificent view (from 3500'–3800') and perhaps some photos, and nobody had to come looking for us. Other points: About what I expected physically demanding ... Two previous entries mention taking dogs up Seward. Either we never got back to the "right" route or you've got some goddamn hard dogs up here. You'd never get any dog with a brain in his head to go up the climb we made. In fact, if I owned a dog who wanted to make that climb, I'd shoot him ... I'd like to tell you where we screwed up—But we don't know!
—SEWARD

Dogs are a convenient scapegoat for some.

I'm on my way back from Dix. Didn't make it to the top. It was much too steep for my dog and I was afraid he was going to have a heart attack before we got to the top. Ran out of water for him too. My two friends were ahead of me when I made the decision (the dog slowed me down a bit). I wonder if I'll ever see them again.

I'm really upset that I couldn't get to the top of Dix. Now I have to wait, probably 2–3 hours for my friends to pass this way later. I guess my dog couldn't make it because I don't run him enough. Learned my lesson, going take him jogging w/me on the Delaware-Raritan Canal when I get back home. He watches too much T.V. and has become a couch potato dog.
—Boquet River

Finally we have the subset of entries from those who are quitting their trip. Discouraged, sore, bitten, they've had enough. Almost always, they are sad, not happy, at the prospect of leaving.

I'm sorry to say I won't be staying. I was on my way to Placid when a little snow fell (2" from Benson to Silver Lake), my feet soaked and froze. After agonizing over whether or not to give up I decided to call it quits. I feel like a failure, but why continue if I'm not enjoying it? What really made it hard was my pack. I weigh 120 and my pack weighs 110 (at least). Well excuses, excuses. I'm off to Rt. 8 to try and thumb a ride home.
—Hamilton Stream

This is a great lean-to; it's just too bad we won't be staying here. Our feet feel like @&<!! after the 10.5 mile hike on*

road from Carry Lean-to this morning. We've killed more mosquitoes than the population of Idaho since our start on July 17. Dog-tired, wet, muddy, sick of bugs, it looks like we'll be completing the trail some other summer. Tomorrow we are hightailing it toward Lake Durant where hot food and dry clothes await us.
—STEPHENS POND

Spent the night at Whitehouse. Second night out from Upper Benson. Breaking trail from Rock Lake has broken me. I think it's into Piseco and a hitch back to my car. When you are alone it is very intense solitude. Maybe I'll succeed at this end to end someday. This is my second try. I decided to try winter to avoid the bugs.
—HAMILTON STREAM

Note that even in their absence, the bugs rule the Adirondacks!

18

Cultures Clash

Drove in here with my three wheeler, shotgun & a couple of cases of Bud ... killin' stuff. I'll kill you too if'n you don't watch out.
— WALLFACE

FOR VIRTUALLY EVERY MAJOR ISSUE in the Adirondacks, there is an argument carried on in the pages of the registers. Hunters vs. nonhunters; motorized vs. nonmotorized access; you name it, people will argue about it. Interestingly, there is relatively little argument over national or international issues. Lean-to debates cover territory close to home.

Some of the most heated debates concern hunting. Many lean-tos are used by hunters during the fall months. Some bring in loads of gear and outfit them as cabins for extended stays. This of course raises the ire of hikers who had hoped to find shelter in the lean-tos.

There is a school of thought that hunters are particularly responsible for trashing lean-tos, but the truth is you can find them trashed pretty much year-round (the lean-tos that is). It's true that more than one register sports a bullet hole or two, but the preponderance of hunter entries express deep reverence for the woods. However, as in this mild example, hunters do put up with a lot of abuse in the registers.

It's a beautiful spot here at Tirrell Pond, but it sure is disappointing that big groups of hunters are flown in to camp here to kill bears and deer. It's impossible to escape the "real world" even in the woods. Too bad.
—TIRRELL POND

The disagreements aren't limited to hunting. A quick tour of Adirondack issues, as presented in the registers, starts with logging. Logging on private lands is a mainstay of the Adirondack economy. There are those who believe it also should be allowed on State land, and that by not doing so, the Adirondack forests are becoming progressively less diverse and healthy.

Lunch Stop. I hate how our society pits one group against another while the fat cats watch unmolested from the sidelines. Today, I've been meditating on how environmentalist and loggers are seen as adversaries—sure our interests are unique, but not totally dissimilar. Like the Native Americans before us, there was a need to harvest wood and create pastures and fields. At the same time, they knew that they had to respect the land so that their children could live off the land as well. Today, however, instead of one person holding both these truths dear, one holds the truth of the need to harvest, the other to preserve—here's where the fat cats take the opportunity to exploit the dichotomy.

The media, logging corporations say it's the Environment vs. Jobs (I'm sick of this). Its that way because the developers have spoiled our autocivilization everywhere with each home sitting on a 1–2 acre lot and paper prices held at artificially low levels (below real costs). We could nurture value-added jobs in the North Country by stimulating the processing of recycled paper and protect more woodland by raising the paper prices to reflect real costs. But these changes hurt timber barons ultimately. Aye ... there's the rub! We must continue to struggle against the excess

consumerism that fattens the pockets of CEO's and lays waste to our mother earth. The moral: Whoever doesn't get enough junk mail should move to another planet.
—BLUEBERRY

In the early 1990s, New York State attempted to reintroduce lynx to the Adirondacks. Thirty-some animals were trapped in the Yukon Territory and released deep in the Adirondack wilderness. The effort to create a breeding population failed. As these entries illustrate, it was not without controversy.

Hi Lynx Fans, I'm up here scent marking the area in anticipation of the lynx release in the next day or so. Beautiful— hope the lynx like the area and hang around. Well off to "scent."
—COLD RIVER 3

The response in the next entry:

Does Lynx restoration really strive to achieve an original, balanced Adirondack ecosystem or is it merely an effort aimed to improve "our impression" of that fleeting, misused word "wilderness"? P.S. Same goes for the spotted owl in Washington State!
—COLD RIVER

Until 1993 there were no rules governing mountain bicycle use on State-owned trails in the Adirondacks. These entries from that year indicate the conflict that led to the designation of trails suitable for this use.

Keegan, John, and Doug.
We unlike some other people
rode our mountain bikes. It was a great trail for us

men, and it is very beautiful.
—CARRY

The next entry:

I can't believe you actually rode these trails. People like you ruin the trails and get us real mountain bikers closed out. All I saw was skids and tracks through deep mud. Wise up!!
—CARRY

Horses and their riders get their turn.

The horse packer guide … is a complete asshole. And we met a horse packer who had a wagon containing tons of shit gear and a chainsaw (not allowed in wilderness), and the red-necked, local town had the audacity to accuse "hikers" of cutting trees to post a trail up Calkins Creek.
—COLD RIVER

Some bad-tempered folks even take issue with the simple advice left by the lean-to adopter at the beginning of the register. The following was written in response to the usual language at the beginning of the Rock Pond register encouraging visitors to keep a clean site and carry out what they had carried in.

Too bad lean to adopters have such a negative attitude—it's one thing to be educational but another to be overly confrontational. Don't need your verbal pollution. I can understand how upsetting it must be when you put so much time and effort into doing something positive but please don't alienate the people on your own shoe.
   This site will be left in better shape than when we arrived—who could ask for more? If we lose our food to bears, we'll pay for it. No one else—but it hasn't happened in 20 years of camping all over the Adirondacks. Never seen

Porkies around here either. You guys must be from Vermont.

I wouldn't mind if all the lean-tos were torn down—they are all a nonconforming structure in the "wilderness"— then we wouldn't have people leaving their trash here. In closing [finally!] where there's use there will be abuse—so don't get steamed—use your energy positively—things are better than they used to be.
—ROCK POND

The lean-to adopter program was founded by ADK in cooperation with the DEC. Here's a DEC staffer annoyed at ADK for, in his view, hogging all the credit!

Lets get the record straight. ADK does a lot of work in the Adirondacks, but not all! This site is frequently patrolled by the DEC and it irks me to no end that people do not realize the efforts of those who break their backs to keep the area clean who work for the DEC. I do not care to be thanked or praised but if you are going to thank some one thank the right people.
—KLONDIKE

After hunters, ATVs inspire the most animated discussion.

ATTENTION lovers of the Middle Branch. This is a forest red alert. At the invitation of NYSDEC we've been invaded by 4-wheelers. Aldrich Pond Wild Forest has been opened to motorized use while 4-wheelers are still illegal elsewhere on State Forest. The rangers couldn't control the illegal use so DEC has made the problem go away by making it legal.

Sound scary? Check out the Long Pond/Mud Creek Trail for an idea of what these machines can do to the land and streams. Unless muddy ruts, loud motors, and helmeted men yelling Yahoo are your idea of a quality forest experience—join forces with eco-minded hikers in opposition to 4-

wheeler use of the State Forest Preserve. Long live activism—FOREST WARRIOR SOCIETY.
—STREETER LAKE

Although rare, they have their defenders.

If it wasn't for the 4-wheelers there would be no trail. The State doesn't do a damn thing.
—CHUB POND

Jet-skis show up now and then.

[Jet skis] are one of the many Personal Wilderness Assault Vehicles now popular among the hordes of Americans that are too lazy and stupid to do anything under their own power. Machines have become a way of life—extensions of the human body (now dehumanized) and thieves of the spirit. How many places are left that are free from the whine and rumbling of motors, the idiot robots that drive them, and the clamor of industrial civilization? How many of us are free?
—TROUT POND

No discussion of cultural or political issues would be complete without dragging things down to a personal level.

The screaming families hiked over to the rock in the water to the left of the point—leaving a trail of cigarette butts. Then they started shooting a pistol around 6:30—The woods can be such a wonderful place sometimes. Around 8:45 they all started crashing over this way—used privy—and hiked out with flashlights—I guess. Good—who the hell needs butt smoking, firearms toten', Skoal chewin', sister lovin', I'm the NRA. Hank Williams, Lyle, Travis country music (added: and ski-doo ridin', 4-wheelin', Garth in

*Central Park, PBR drinkin') car up on blocks, pollutin',
rednecks out here anyway.*
—STEPHENS POND

Speaking of screeds, here's the all-time champion. What
didn't this guy find to complain about?

*Your trail guides are useless; at 12 dollars they're outra-
geous. Any trail more than 5 miles long is continued in
another book.*

    *Don't build any bridges here Dave. Between you and the
DEC you have managed to destroy the high peaks. You
made it so easy for people to get through there that people
who couldn't find their way down the street are going 15
miles back. You don't need a bridge over every little muddy
spot and creek. Perhaps if you tore down some of the bridges
the wimps would find out that they don't like fording and
then they would stay closer to the road. Then you might be
able to find room to pitch a tent at the Opalescent, and that
girl might not have tried to climb Colden during the winter
(the one who got killed) if she had to ford creeks during the
winter.*

    *I wonder if you need a building permit for a foot bridge?
Is it in good keeping with forever wild to be doing this? You
people should be more concerned about acid rain and less
about getting your boots dirty.*

    *The DEC says there's no fish above 2000 feet, how long
before the acid moves down stream? 1 year maybe 2 years?
I think it already has before they even finished their
research.*

    *I'm making the loop from Otter Brook. You have to ford
2 creeks to make the loop. By the looks of the trail register
it keeps a lot of people out. Last year only about 6 or 7
groups made this loop. Half of them will probably not come
back. Why don't you just cut down the trees so we can see
the woods better?*

They are talking about charging a fee for a permit to camp in the Adirondacks. That's okay but remember that the NYS residents are footing the bill already. Charge the nonresidents extra. The people from NJ come up here pay nothing for it and then bitch about the trail conditions. If you want easy trails stay in NJ you already destroyed all the woods there. The Canadians come down here and hike all they want but they charge us $500 for a Canadian fishing license. Enough bitching for one day. [Not hardly ...]

Oh, does the DEC realize that by killing black flies they are destroying the trout's food? And is that pile of shit next to the rangers cabin set an example for how clean we should be? I've seen bear tracks and dung back here to.

The guy who's complaining about only catching one brookie shouldn't consider himself unfortunate. I've yet to catch a single fish back here in two years. I'm a lousy fisherman anyway but I should at least catch something with the amount of stocking they do to these lakes. Yes, they are stocked, they drop them from an airplane.

Whoever the idiot is who likes to sleep on the cedar branches please clean up the mess when done—the needles are a pain in the ass (literally) when they dry up. If you use the firewood that's left in the lean to please replace it, it's nice to have some dry wood to start a fire when it's raining. Memorial Day, Radio says Emerson Fittipaldi won Indy.
—WEST CANADA LAKE

There were lots and lots of replies, although none were nearly as entertaining.

There is a class of entries that revolves around the Forest Preserve itself. Oddly, some of those using it don't think it should exist.

1st overnight stop for Hike Against Big Government. Three hikers, hiking to increase awareness of the oppressive gov-

ernment. Hiking to cut taxes, reduce bureaucracy, enhance individual liberty, and encourage self-reliance. "The government that governs least governs best." Great shelter, super view.
—MOOSE POND

The reply.

In reference to May 15 entry, "Hike Against Big Government": Government is what made the Adirondack Park and its beauty possible. Formerly, it was completely denuded by timber companies. Unfortunately, Government, as collectors of our taxes, is the only thing that can save the Adirondack Park, by purchasing the private land within its boundaries it is now in minimal danger of destructive development. We usually get the government we deserve. Let yours speak for you. Tell your NY State Senator you want your tax dollars to protect the Adirondack Park. End of political speech. Breathe the air.
—MOOSE POND

Management of Forest Preserve lands is a topic of never-ending discussion, with particular emphasis on the "Forever Wild" provision of the New York State Constitution.

This used to be a nice place until someone had the great idea to get rid of the ranger who took care of the woods like it was their own back yard. Now it is Forever Wild and Forever a Mess!
—CEDAR LAKES 1

Interestingly, Mario Cuomo, governor of New York from 1983 to 1994 and generally considered a friend of the Forest Preserve, gets it from both sides.

Snowmobiled in. Nice to see our tax money so well and conspicuously spent. Trail in bad shape, many trees down perhaps due to loss of Mario Cuomo—too bad. Maybe now woods can go (revert) back to formerly inaccessible & pristine nature. Lean-to is great—probably cost $100,000 tax money. Local carpenter could have done it for $1800. Thank God the liberals are gone, gone, gone.
—BURNTBRIDGE POND

It's too bad that Mario Cuomo is from N.Y.C.; maybe if he got out of the city he could appreciate something as beautiful as this. But don't count on it. It's unfortunate that N.Y. State doesn't consider the Adirondacks one of its most valuable resources. Anyway, sorry about the pissing and moaning, thanks to anyone who has made this place as it is.
—FISH POND 1

There are even those who are opposed to the relatively few (and sensible) rules society has had the good sense to pass to protect the wilderness.

8/24/91 Swam in the pond. Thank God <u>that's</u> not against the rules yet (see inside front cover of register). Probable rules eight years from now:

No camping near anything
Don't touch nothing
No smiling nor talking
Must apply for entry permit (in triplicate) two years in advance & if we "lose" it, too bad.
No complaining!
—WOLF POND

Finally, we have those who are annoyed with all the arguing and wish everybody would just shut up.

I enjoyed reading many of the entries and lovely poems in this notebook as I sit in the shelter of this comfortable lean-to. I did not at all appreciate, however, the individuals who saw this book as an opportunity to impose their opinions on meat-eaters, fat hairy females and vodka. This is not the city folks, so lets get our minds out of the gutter.
—PHARAOH

Loud rushing of a nearby stream,
Damp woodsy smell of rotting leaves,
Let us dream of better things:
A world of peace and dignity.
Where clean air and water are reality
Where men can live with other men
No war, no hunger, nor poverty.
Oh fresh breeze cleanse our hearts,
And high peaks lift our souls,
So we may reach our journey's end
And live the way we ought to live.

8/16/88
—LILLIAN BROOK

19

Huntin' and Fishin'

Willing to trade daughter for can of worms. See Tom at Turtle Canyon.
—STONY POND

LOTS OF FISHING ENTRIES in the registers. Big fish, little fish, many fish, no fish. Historically, the Adirondacks offered great fishing. Accounts from the mid-nineteenth century abound with ponds full of five-pound trout that jumped into the fisherman's creel to escape the overcrowding. The overpopulation problem has been solved, but the fish are still there if you know what you are doing. Many don't.

Our plan is falling apart. Our attempt to live off the fat of the land is failing miserably. We have spent 10 person days trying to catch a fish using lures, worms, newts, frogs & rocks for bait. Nada! Will give up trying to catch a fish. Setting snares this afternoon for bears, moose, bigfoot (bigfeet), etc. Hope we won't starve.
—PHARAOH LAKE 1

Scenery great; fishing sucks. If I wanted to see something as small as the three trout we caught, I'd take a leak. I'm glad we also brought sandwiches for lunch. Funny, the guy at the tackle shop told us this place was great, sold us $20 worth of

spoons and said he comes here often. Bullshit. At least it's pretty.
—OXSHOE POND

For the fisherman, the registers function to impart local information.

Whoever stops by to fish, if you catch anything please write down what it was. And what kind of bait you used. We trolled a Lake Clear Wobbler for 4.5 hours. No luck. Try fishing the cove to your left. We saw a lot of fish jump in there. Good Luck!
—CLEAR POND

Personally, I can't imagine telling the run of the public where the good spots are so they can be fished out, but some see it differently.

In for a couple of days of secluded fall trout fishing. Worked Grassy Brook on Monday plus a little of the Cedar River. On Tuesday worked a two-mile stretch at the W Canada Creek below Mud Lake. Was using dry flies though I did manage to catch 5 trout in the 4" to 6" range and one strong 8" fish. Returned all fish except the chubs which became 'coon food.

Remember if you really want trout for dinner use earthworms and #6 or 8 hooks weighted with split shot. May, June, and Sept best months.
—WEST CANADA LAKE

We've been camping here three days & are moving on to the campsite @ Sucker Brook—We recommend it; the brook runs steady & you may catch some brookies. If you have boat, float down to the hole @ the far east end of the lake for a great sunrise view—this is the end of the lake to see the sun set behind the mountain to your west. Lake trout can be found about 200' this side of the camp—there is an 80' "bowl" in that area where they prefer to swim. [Name of lean-to withheld by the author, who has his principles to uphold.]

For a number of years the DEC has been poisoning certain ponds with the pesticide rotenone, the purpose being to remove whatever fish are present so that brook trout can be introduced. The process is not without controversy. Rotenone leaves an ugly aftermath as it kills most life in the pond. Furthermore, most such ponds will eventually need to be re-treated if a trout fishery is to be maintained. The practice is particularly offensive to those with no interest in trout fishing. Protesters have gone so far as to assault officers applying the pesticide.

The wise men are trying to reclaim this beautiful lake. They have put "toxicants" in the water. You can smell the poison. There is a death spirit pervading the whole area. Dead fish are floating in the water. My brother and I don't understand. We have said prayers to protect ourselves and this beautiful land. The dead fish are catfish. If you fish and catch a catfish & cook its meat, it is very tasty. Trout on the other hand are tasty too. What's the difference?
—OXSHOE POND

I have fished this pond for ten years. It was the greatest trout water I ever fished. Then two or three years ago DEC decided to kill all the brook trout and restock it with rainbows. I haven't caught a fish since. Thanks a lot.
—FISHBROOK POND 2

Occasionally you will see a supportive entry.

Just came by on a short day hike us being myself, wife and 11-month old son. Weather just perfect today—sunny about 50°. Read all about horrors of re-claiming pond but if no one would bring in bait fish not native to this pond, one would not have to re-claim pond—next spring all will be good again and hopefully the rest of us will keep it that way and enjoy this area for years to come.
—*OXSHOE POND*

A few years ago I got the bright idea of bringing an inflatable raft into West Lake, a hike of about seven miles. The lake is fairly large and reputed to have good fishing at one time. Given its remoteness, I figured I'd be the only boat on it in years. Things I learned from this experiment:

1. Inflatable boats add a lot of weight to your pack, but a plastic paddle makes a handy hiking stick.

2. No matter how anxious you are to fish, don't try to blow the boat up immediately after a seven-mile hike if you want to remain conscious.

3. It's pretty much impossible to control a small raft in a lake as big as West in even the smallest breeze, to say nothing of trying to fish from it.

4. The fishing is no longer very good in West, as confirmed by this next entry.

I first came here in 1970. Many things have changed over the years. The ranger station arose there; nice old ranger retired from here and that year they stocked the lake with many and big trout. Those days they allowed flying parties into the lake and they had rowboats for rent. You talk about garbage; people brought in everything and all garbage was left here. I'm sure some garbage you see is from that era. Its rather ironic but they had big signs up not to use live minnows for they were afraid of contaminating the lake with

tramp species. I think the lake was acidic then but it wasn't recognized. The stocked trout survived but couldn't propagate. What is the pH of the lake now? Each year I remember all the details to pack but forgot some litmus paper in pH from 4.5 to 7.0. Would it really make any difference if I knew? It is a lovely place but it could be even better.
—West Canada Lake

As already noted, there are a fair number of anti-hunting entries: *Was going to cut north of Stephens but heard a sequence of 19 shots. Figured Stephens is one of my favorite places so I'd stop by to see that Swiss Deer. Stephens Pond.* However, the registers also have a handful of thoughtful entries from hunters who have been coming to a place a long time and whose respect for the land is obvious.

11/5 "Jack Buck" Hunting Club arrived today. Camp was in excellent shape. A good bit of trash out of the fire pit but overall camp is very clean. Although we are apparently "Dreaded Hunters" I'm sure we will leave this camp as "<u>real woodsmen</u>" would. It's great to be back!! Only one brief glimpse of a tail today.

11/6 Rain, rain and yes even more rain. No deer or bear seen today but I saw a pair of Pileated Woodpeckers hard at work. Yesterday during a drive three does were kicked back towards me. They ran up to within 30 feet of me before they saw me. It was very exciting and worth this week of rain. Remember it is the adventure of the hunt not the kill which is most exciting.

11/7 The end of our 1989 adventure. No deer or bear harvested this year but we look forward to coming back. As we attempt to be the cleanest nature conscious campers it hurts our pride to be the dreaded ones. But life goes on.
—O'Neil Flow

Hiked in from High Falls on 3rd day of hunting trip. Rained the whole day and on through the night but glad temp warmed up from −5F, the weekend low. Saw very little sign in the High Falls Plains/Little Shallow area and we are hoping for better luck here.

Tuesday. Snow in the morning and temperature in the 20's. Hunted hills east of shelter and south of lake. Snow heavy at times, returned cold and wet in the afternoon, and ventured north on the logging road toward Wanakena in the evening. So far, we've seen beaver and mice, but no big game.

Wednesday. Hunted up toward Glasby Pond and found a lot of tracks. Went up Cat Mountain in heavy snowfall and then on to Cat Mountain Pond, picking up an occasional track but no deer yet. Enjoying pepperoni and cheese for lunch, along with assorted nuts and raisins. Snow finally abated near dark, and we built a big fire which was thoroughly appreciated by both of us.

Thursday. 1st real nice day of trip. Partly cloudy. Temps in the 20's, snow depth 4–5 inches. After the typical oatmeal, we headed off toward Cat Mountain Lake again and decided to follow some frozen tracks heading south. After about 2 hours of this we decided to head back toward the trail and began to hunt northwest. Heavy beaver activity necessitated several detours around swamps and we found ourselves lost and in the dark. We finally found our way out by compass and flashlight up the Leary Trail and into Wanakena. We trudged back down to Janecks and got in around 8:30. We promptly collapsed into our bags, exhausted but warm and happy.

The beavers around here are hellacious. Some areas are

 *very nearly impassable and necessitate crawling through downed trees and swamps. Beginning to culture*

a hearty dislike for the animals. A week of deer hunting and all we've seen is a few tracks, 1 beaver, a fishing crane, some bold insects and a mouse. The area is beautiful, but the deer hunting is better in my back yard.

Today we stayed in camp all day, stoked the fire & ate (resting up from yesterday's ordeal). Tomorrow to Wanakena and back home.

—JANECKS LANDING

20

Companions

What sick desire could drive a person to drag their spouse and children through the mud and rain and cold and wind from early morn till into the dark?
—*KLONDIKE*

THE ENTRIES IN CHAPTER 22 notwithstanding, most people hike and camp with others: family, friends, scouts, and sundry ad hoc collections like summer camps and freshman bonding trips. My experience with the latter was that a sort of social stratification similar to high school quickly asserted itself, but this group seemed to like one another.

The green of the leaves hold more gold than dollar bills. About 1 p.m. and we really should start climbing this crazy mountain—Dix. I am afraid: I am afraid, of running out of breath, of falling into nowhere, of digging it too much to write that paper Monday night. So if you hear 2 women laughing loud on the top of Dix you'll know it was me.

So who is with me? Well there's Carla sitting next to me—I believe she's the youngest one at the tender age of 18 (but she'll soon be 20) she's sort of city but more country at heart I believe. Then there's David from Oneonta, camera man, soft spoken but joking around, but that's just a first impression I met him yesterday, Carl, Long Islander who jokes like a grandfather and

makes the best scrambled eggs in the soft morning we just finished. Joe—Guisseppe—barefoot boy—screaming of cold water and trees—makes good fires and laughs like a river. And Kris coffee goddess, patron saint of the national romantic mind—eyes like the pith of a tree.

We are here from New Paltz, kids loose in a forest, flash-lights dimming, orange-juice disappearing, screaming laughing, laughing, laughing. Watching with large inno-cent eyes the odor of autumn seep in and take over ...
—LILLIAN BROOK

During July and August the woods are crawling with the inevitable boy scouts, who fill the register pages with their observations. I will spare you these gems of insight, which are mainly focused on the bodily functions of the members of their tribe.

A series of registers from the same lean-to will sometimes contain sequential entries from a group making its annual visit. Often the members are in their early twenties, and often they give themselves nicknames. (My annual camp-ing trip at this age was as a member of the Smith Mountain Lake Baseball Association, a sort of cross between an outing club and a baseball convention.) The Cinchbuggers visited Stephens Pond for a number of years.

Cinchbuggers, Inc. It was sad to learn of the missing dart board. It brought many great memories (since '92). Nobody was "leached" this year, although one swimmer sure did come close. We had a successful game of Frisbee (ultimate). We witnessed a loon fight as an intruder landed between parents and their young. The adults chased and screamed at the bird till it was a half-mile down the lake.

Our first neighbor was from Northville. "Titanium Man" humored us with his unique (?/@#/) character. He even shared his refreshment (gin and Prestone II). Only a stogie (White Fowl) could remove the smell.

We visited the cave just down the trail and played Frisbee inside the main chamber (OK, so we just crawled inside). We had a raccoon gnawing our low-slung food bag. He did not like the apple juice, so left the rest for us.

This was the Cinchbuggers 10th Anniversary Stephens Pond Campout. Over the years we've had numerous incidents including the "Butt Boils" from New Jersey, the MAD hacker, and wonderful Hackey Sack incidents. We also had only one bear incident over the ten years. The fire is out and its time to go. Cinchbuggers '95.

—STEPHENS POND

Part of lean-to culture involves sharing space with people who have different, um, habits than you. The following entry is a brief excerpt from a screed that went on (and on) for many pages.

Hiked in yesterday from Round Pond. Had a wonderful hike up Dix (solo). A couple of loud "campers" behind me inspired me to make tracks. This was of course right at the base of the slide with the unrelenting climb. I managed to lose the offenders ... the cost? My heart rate was at 180 when standing still ... and lost a lot of water breathing and sweating.

Dix was beautiful although haze and clouds obscured complete views. Met wonderful people on top ... real hikers ... respectful of nature and solitude. Took their photo for them. We were soon interrupted by ... oh noooo ... the OFFENDERS! We heard them coming from probably 1/4 mile. When within 20 yards they seemed to delight in informing us that we weren't on "the summit" (no fooling?). They clambered over to the summit and proceeded to rattle off the names of all surrounding peaks for all to benefit from. After a 10 min. stop, they headed back down. Now they can say they hiked Dix.

—BOQUET RIVER

Then there are the companions you weren't too sure about, but end up liking.

Arrived at falls … when we got here a backpacker was here. Later a "Jack" came down from the falls. Seems to know camping but talks and laughs a lot to himself. Guess this'll be an interesting night. Seems a lot like clients I used to work with at K.E.Y.
—WANIKA FALLS

The next day's entry read: *And so Jack goes on. Not a burden, but a free man making' it the best he can. We talked of the Iliad and the ascent of man, food and rain.*

And there are the companions you're glad *aren't* here.

What a beautiful day. Sun shining. Little breeze. Saw loons out in the middle of the pond. Three boys are having a ball catching minnows. Am really enjoying the peace and quiet here. Wife left with another man five weeks ago. Really needed this! Glad she's not here, would ruin another fine day.
—STONY POND

Some of my favorite entries illustrate the joys and burdens of camping with loved ones. Especially fun are entries written by kids.

Hi, I'm Amanda and I'm here with my family and we are thinking of staying for five days. The trip in was hard because we had these great big hiking packs and they were heavy. We had to walk out to get all the food we had to leave behind because we did not have room or the strength to carry it all. So in all we walked nine miles. The only problems were the beaver dams with the great big bags.

But we're glad we went through all the trouble because the view is nice. The lean-to is in nice condition and the

bathroom was OK too. The water was very warm so we went swimming. The rocks were slimy but we managed.
—WOLF LAKE

We are here from Hopewell New Jersey, on a 1-week camping trip. We've decided to move here—my dad says he will write a novel while my sister and I (aged 7 and 10) go to work to support the family. We will cut wood, baby-sit, and wash cars while my dad waits for a "big idea" to come. He says it will certainly not be more than 2 winters before he has at least an idea for the book.

The thing is, my father is not even a writer—he's an architect. And we can't be sure that 2 years of washing cars will be enough for him to think of something. He says that writing must be easier than making buildings—and he wanted to redesign this lean-to but we stopped him. We'll probably be back here again—probably forever—so we'll let you know what happens to us.
—CARRY

Especially moving are entries telling of companions who are no longer here.

Dear Mom, The last time I was here was when we came here together about 4 years ago. Remember, we took a wrong turn somewhere along the trail and stumbled upon Cascade Pond. It was our lucky day! Now you are hiking in paradise and I've got to make do with our little paradise here. Your spirit is the wind in the trees. I thank God for this day!
—STEPHENS POND

This weekend, Sean, Ian and I hiked in here to scatter the ashes of Roland C.—Ian's father, and a "father figure" for Sean and myself (and many others). Roland was a ranger at Shattuck Clearing in the 1960's. He loved this region tremendously, and he made a point to share its stories with his closest friends and family. He loved to bring us up here. Roland's life philosophy was basically to "fuck it"—to not worry about petty social rules and rituals. He liked to "just do" his job and then to have the best time possible.

Roland died July 26, 1993 of a disease similar to leukemia called multiple myeloma. He was only 54. Some of us have speculated that it was a result of DDT used here in the 60's. In any case, we have written an "in memory" to Roland on the right hand side of the lean-to—on the vertical log facing the river. We ask all who read this to go over it with some charcoal from their fires to prevent it from fading. We also ask that all who read this to "fuck it" now and then, and that they have a great time while they're here—in Roland's honor—We will come back as often as we can and do the same. Thank you.

—COLD RIVER 4

Hello—Streeter Lake
Baby Jo-Jo's first visit
First camping trip had to
Be in this special nature place

Joey didn't know what to think
About bein' close up in Daddy's
Tent so he looked up and down,
And all around—then he howled

Oh—Daddy—I want out
Was the message sent without
So many words said—go down
To the lake light Jo-Jo
And daddy went

Joey pointed high in the east
To where the Evening Star
Sparkled—he wanted Daddy
To see

Out on the dark lake
Something moved on silver reed
Not enough light to be seen
But daddy knows who—
Gotta' be three Streeter Lake loons

I saw the silver wakes and swimming
Bird outlines, dim and close in
The near dark
Then the next morning, the mated
Pair and one young of the year
Glided back and forth past me
On the lakeshore
Being companionable, making
Gentle clucking sounds
Their silver wakes intermeshing
Harmoniously

Time to go—Baby Jo-Jo
Bye-Bye Streeter Lake
Bye-Bye moon
Bye-Bye shooting stars
Bye-Bye loons
Joey's first camping trip is over but that's okay
'cause we'll all be back soon

—STREETER LAKE

157

21

Religion

There is no God. But there are a hell of a lot of frogs.
—STEPHENS POND

I GUESS THE PLACE where philosophy ends and religion begins is right about here: Is there a God, and if so, what's His or Her story? For a lot of hikers, the natural world holds the answer. Register comments can be broadly divided into three schools of thought: 1) There is no God, but there is this here beautiful natural world, so quit yer worryin' and enjoy it; 2) Nature is God and God is Nature, so enjoy; and 3) God made all this for you to enjoy; be sure to thank Him. Note that all three views are remarkably similar: they all recognize the outstanding beauty and wonder in the natural world; seek to understand it and cannot; and are humbled and amazed by what they see. You'd think that people with so much common ground would get along a little better.

Let the forest
Be salvation
Long before
It needs to be.

—BUSHNELL FALLS 3

We'll start with the tree huggin' nature worshippers.

Halloween (Samhain) Greetings. What better way to say goodbye to the old year and step into a timeless space of serenity and wonder. Thank you wind, water, fire and earth. See you soon.
—HAMILTON STREAM

Next pew over are those for whom the natural world itself is the church.

Sunday ... We are alone with the "silence" of nature. Bugs aren't bad. What's the point in going to church when there is this! Isn't this what "God" wants us to worship? Not some building that men built and mumble in and threaten us all with damnation from! No—this is church ... infinitely complex, self-sustaining, elegant and of course HARMONIOUS. Oh that we humans could be the same.
—High Falls East

A variant is those who are conventionally religious, but who also look on the natural world as a place for worship.

...this is my Rosh Hashanah celebration; today is one of the anniversaries of the birth of the Earth ... better to be here celebrating the creation of God, than in a stuffy house of worship, built by humans, where most people repeat by rote meaningless prayers. The smell of perfumes on attendees in worship can never match the natural perfumes of the woods and river. Thank you Lord! This is the day the Lord has created. Let us be glad and rejoice thereof.
—Griffin Rapids

All faiths are found in the woods. The travels of a Muslim father and his son can be traced in registers from lean-tos on the Oswegatchie River after the microburst storm of 1995. A typical entry reads: *In the name of Allah, most gracious and most merciful, who has shown us all his power in the massive blowdown, and his beauty on this lovely river. Cage Lake Springhole.*

There is a fair amount of mix and match; here, Buddhism and baseball.

Rest stop for my next to last granola bar before finishing up the NPT, 8th day out. While my experience was perhaps not so, er, religious as that of the previous writers, I too enjoyed the trail. Whether you worship the Lord, Allah, Buddha, Rocks, Sticks, Twine or, like me, Willie Mays, I trust you will strive hard to realize the unity of all reality.
—WANIKA FALLS

We move on to those for whom the natural world inspires praise for God as the maker of the beautiful creation surrounding the writer.

The Earth is the Lord's and the fullness thereof. Thou are worthy oh Lord to receive glory and honor, for thou hast created all things! We thank you Jesus for all you have made for us to enjoy!
—WANIKA FALLS

Just came out here to explore and to enjoy the quietness of the woods. The old hemlock, birch and maple along the trail are beautiful ... God deserves much glory for making them.
—INLET FLOW

More dogmatic are those for whom the splendor of the natural world is an ipso facto argument for the existence of God, in this case a Christian God. Perhaps he thought the Muslim God specializes in desert landscapes.

Been nearly 20 years since Lynn and I were here—place hasn't changed much—forest has matured and opened up—trails have deteriorated—sky, wind and water are gorgeous as ever. To all the non-believers: only a Christian God could create such geological wonders, peace and tranquility.
—PHARAOH LAKE 1

Hiked in from Rt. 3—trail had anything from 6–20 inches of snow in many spots. Grueling! Lean-to is fine and view is great! Nature is quite a kick. And yet, what of its incredible design? Don't tell me that all of this is mere chance, some kind of accident. If you consider it deeply you must conclude that this awesome design is the product of an even more awesome designer. "The heavens reveal the glory of God and the firmament showeth forth his handiwork." Psalm 19:1.
—BURNTBRIDGE POND

The preceding entry illustrates a common practice: the recording of scripture. Unlike philosophers, there is no single passage in greatest favor. However, as anyone who has completed a difficult portage knows, it ought to be this one.

From Saranac Lake to Polliwog to Hoel to Turtle to Clamshell to Fish Pond for the night. The carry from Turtle to Clamshell was a Monster Portage. With solo carries I am reminded of a thought, "Rejoice in our sufferings. Because we know that suffering produces perseverance, perseverance character, and character hope." Romans 5:3–4.
—FISH POND 1

But many people do have other explanations. Some of the sharpest, not to say snottiest exchanges in the registers concern religion. Despite all the stated good intentions, religion seems to be a subject that divides as much as it unites.

Today's walk really spoke to me of the complexity, beauty, diversity and vastness of God's creation. And it's all a "Gift." Peace.
—CASCADE POND

The immediate reply in the next entry:

God is dead. But the woods and ponds are lovely. We come every year from Delaware. We have peace and love without God.
—CASCADE POND

I am reading El Salvador in Revival by T. Wynn Drost. The burden for missions is really heavy on me. Note: The way of salvation is repentance, baptism in the name of the Lord Jesus Christ and in the filling of the Holy Ghost with speaking in tongues. Acts 2:4, 38.
—CASCADE POND

Again, the very next entry:

Note: the real way to salvation is: 1) Avoid organized religious activity. 2) Make nature your religion if you must say you have one. 3) Drink beer when appropriate. 4) Have a good time.

The responses above are mild; the entries that attract the most ire are those that proselytize. The margins surrounding an entry recommending religious conversion are nearly always overflowing with passionate reaction. The following entry was preceded by this editorial comment in the margin: *Before you read this next entry, be sure not to have eaten in the past hour, because it's going to make you sick.*

Greetings and salutations … We've had fun out here today and plan on coming back soon. A California boy by birth and residence, this place is breathtaking. But anyways to get to the heart of the matter. If you don't know Jesus Christ as your Lord and Savior you need to make that decision and understand the reality of God and his Son who shed his Blood on a wooden cross so that whoever would believe in him would have the right to become a child of God and

Listening to the loon high pitched
Tone
Sitting around the fire
With my friends as we reminisce
Talking about getting home
And the precious memories we
All miss
Will they ever think back
To the things we went through
How we climbed the high peaks

And spotted the bald eagle and
"ahhhed" as it flew
Maybe we'll meet up
And together watch "our"
Kids play
Then once again we'll
Reminisce
God will bring us together
Again.

—CASCADE POND

God walks in the forest—
Hear him sing!
His voice carries in tiny bubbles throughout the roaring brook.
Ahh the views!

—OULUSKA PASS

spend eternity in heaven with the almighty Creator of the Universe. Please read this literature. Get a hold of a Bible and receive the greatest gift ever offered to man. God Bless.
—CEDAR POINT

The editorializer then followed with: *See what I mean. People like this should be shot to put us out of our misery.*

For the truly committed, even the lean-to adopters are fair game.

To G. K., We have come to know you through your devotion to these lean-tos. You have learned the true secret of servant hood. The bible says if you are going to be great in God's kingdom learn to be the servant of all. Through your work on these lean-tos, you serve everyone who stays in them. A person like you would be great in God's Kingdom. I don't know if you're "born again" or not (though the world has greatly worked over this term), but Jesus is it's author. You will find it in the 3rd chapter of the book of John, 3rd verse (read whole chapter) and Romans 10:9 and 10.

Murray was right in his book "Adventures in the Wilderness." He said a pastor should come here to get renewed and both my wife and I have experienced great renewal of spirit, soul, and body during our stay. What I have told you here has transformed my life from a gun toting, trigger happy prostitute chasing, GI in 1974, to a servant of God, a pastor, who desires to reach out to others. I am now reaching out to you. If you desire to talk to somebody who is "for real" and does not play games with people's lives then please write me.
—COLD RIVER

I have yet to be visited in a lean-to by earnest young men in matching white shirts and ties, but I suppose it's inevitable that it will happen one day.

22

Solitude

Spent day sitting in the marsh watching hummingbirds till lunch and sitting at stream watching water after lunch. Stocked up on quiet to last a while.
—HAMILTON STREAM

OUTDOORS ORGANIZATIONS such as the Adirondack Mountain Club discourage solo camping, and understandably so. The consequences of a sprained ankle are greatly magnified if you are alone. Hiking organizations are occasionally sued by folks who buy their guidebooks and then get lost in the woods. Discouraging solo adventures is an almost inevitable loss-prevention measure for an organization in this position.

With this disclaimer made, many hikers prefer to be in the woods by themselves. I find that after a few days the incessant humming inside my cranium slows down, allowing clear observation of what is going on around me. As I begin to see the world without the noise and mental static of "civilization," my thought process sharpens. Judging from the registers, many others have a similar experience.

There are lots of reasons people go into the woods alone. One of the most common is finding the quiet to work out a problem of some sort. The registers are full of entries from people who have come to the forest for contemplation, or in the case of this entry, remembrance.

Two weeks ago, on Aug. 16, Ken & I were to leave on a 23-day whitewater canoe trip on the South Nahanni River in the Northwest Territories in Canada. Ken did not show up at LaGuardia, and we missed the flight. When I went over to his house, I found him in bed. He had had a heart attack and died the night before. He was 44.

After the funeral, I decided I had to come out here alone. I've been out for 6 days so far, trying to sort things out. Being here at Wanika Falls really helps a lot. The beauty & solitude are very therapeutic. Thanks to Joyce, Gary & all those who have passed through for helping to maintain this pristine location. And thank you, Ken, for sharing so many outdoor experiences.
—WANIKA FALLS

A not uncommon entry is from someone using the peaceful woods as a setting in which to make a decision.

I'm saying goodbye early this year. Deciding not to <u>endure.</u> Endure in a way of life. Deciding I <u>will</u> join the commerce of other human beings if I can (you see, Putnam Pond is

my yearly experiment at being a hermit). Practical sessions so to speak and this has been a profound year of disconnection (6 months teaching phys Ed in NYC, East Harlem—But so much disconnection even with millions around). Loneliness just knows no bounds. Sure I'm in some pain. But isn't that what the woods are for too? And I never forget to look at the color and notice

the changes in the water surface, sleek and smooth. And I laughed out loud this morning when I heard scooping nois- es, like a cartoon of a jet. And it turned out, in the silence, to be 4 ducks circling in for a landing.
—Grizzle Ocean

Not everyone is into being alone. Some try it, but find they are lonely and apprehensive.

My first trip backpacking and supposedly I have wandered into the finest lean-to in the Adirondacks. I have done a lot of camping—usually from a hike—but never alone. This will be my first night alone—in the woods. I was afraid I wouldn't be able to find a lean-to w/some available space— I was both pleased and concerned when I found this one vacant. Will I be able to sleep at all? Or will I think every noise is that of a bear? Once the sun goes down I will be completely at the hands of fate—may she be kind!
—Klondike

But solitude isn't scary or intimidating for those who open their eyes to what's happening around them.

Sunny, beautiful to color the hillside. Spent a beautiful night here, had the lake to ourselves with the exception of 3 loons, 6 mergansers, 1 blue heron, 1 kingfisher, ruffed grouse, black beaked woodpecker, barred owl, solitary and red eyed, 6 kinds of warblers, cedar waxwing, 1 thrush, 7 ducks flying overhead, and small mammals running over the shelter roof at night. Bob the Bear absent. Just a few frogs and tiny fish in water, bat cruising through for insects. Could stay a month!
—West Canada Lake

The converse of solitude is that sometimes it's just too darn crowded in the woods.

Came in on the 12th lucky enough to get this great lean-to as a family of five was just leaving. Had a great day Friday the 12th then till about 3:30 on Saturday as we had the lake to ourselves with only the loons as company. Then they came. By fours by twos by twos and by fours. Before you knew what was going on twelve people set up camp within spitting distance of the lean-to. You couldn't turn around without bumping into somebody. Good thing we came out here to get away from things. Should have gone to Woodstock 2.
—MIDDLE SETTLEMENT LAKE

Spend enough time in the woods and you'll have an experience like that above. These events are more than offset by the amazing, renewing power of the woods.

Sunny, peaceful, quiet, about 65 degrees. Pungent smell of nature baking in the sun. More tranquil than a fist full of Valium. The mind washing serenity of this place leaves me in awe of Mother Nature and her beautiful gifts she gives us for the taking. I'm glad I had time to stop, look and smell the beauty. Nothing compares!
—STEPHENS POND

For me, the best thing about being alone is that you can slow down and listen to your heart as well as the world around you. Both have truths to tell you that you need to hear.

As I walked by the Cold River this morning miles went by, and I came to the suspended bridge. Already over, I went on. Next step—the lake—but the sun is out, and it's early … this little engine inside me was saying go, go further, faster… And I said NO … I went back. HERE. About a mile … Stop the clock … Live. I feel it's a great victory for me. Maybe it'll seem silly to you. I'll be 29 on the 29th, two

days from now. Richer and wiser! Thanks to the Cold River.
—COLD RIVER 3

The silence of the woods inspires pithy entries with a Zen quality.

Today I hike along the trail—contemplating the silent competition of the trees. Buggy walk in wet woods. Short paddle in leaky boat. Bold chipmunk in the lean-to. Warm fire in my mind.
—STEPHENS POND

Spooky, frozen quietude. This can be marketed more profitably than lumber.
—OXSHOE POND

9:20 p.m. Light drizzle. We made a great meal and the fire is raging and we are having a great time. How beautiful it is to hear mother earth in its normalcy.
—STEPHENS POND

Take a few breaths, sit and listen to the falls and allow all your worries to float away.
—HIGH FALLS EAST

A final entry that nicely summarizes what many of these entries are trying to say.

It has taken me a few hours to write thus far. I've rested my pen here and there to chat with other hikers passing through, and also to get up and stretch and breathe the mountain air, to listen to the sounds that Mother Earth emits. I am learning that solitude is a way towards Peace of Mind. The philosophers from centuries past have said it. Emerson has said it, Whitman and Thoreau. Anyone who has acquired a certain amount of higher knowledge knows that they owe everything to quiet attentiveness and patient reflection.

The higher we climb the steps of knowledge the more necessary is this quiet listening. All perceptions of truth, all action and life in the world of the spirit are delicate in comparison with the functions of the ordinary intellect and the business of life in the physical world. The wider our horizon becomes the more delicate are the activities we have to undertake. It is absolutely correct that truth and the higher life abide in every human soul and that each individual can and must find them for himself. But they are deeply buried and can be brought up from the depths only after all obstacles have been cleared away.

—CASCADE POND

THE LURE OF SOLITUDE

I like to see these mountains
All alone
Without the reminder
Of what is home
Like people
And cars
And movies
And bars
Money can't burn
Where fires don't turn.
Civilization entrenches the mind
Into rooms
And boxes
Whereas nature confronts
Oneself
With what is real.

—CEDAR POINT

Branches burdened
Heavy and white
Only three miles deep
I feel light years away
From thought and worry
Responsibility and duty
Soul cleansed
Mind empty
My shoulders are light
The weight of my
Pack, that's all.
40 lbs., I'll take that any day
Over power windows, coffee stirrers,
Oil filters, nagging boss, weight loss
Clinics, Dept. stores, radial tires,
Light bulbs, bulletin boards, asphalt,
Gravel pits, detergent, refrigerators
And misc. other effects
That tend to clutter one's life
One's stream of thought.
Live.
Dream.

—CASCADE POND

23

Satori

Solvitor Ambulando! (In walking it is solved.)
—OULUSKA PASS

YOU WOULD EXPECT the registers to be filled with philosophical discourse, and they are. Much of it is predictable, and so what. The most interesting entries are nearly always found in the registers from the most remote parts of the Forest Preserve: The Five Ponds, the West Canada Lakes, the Cold River country.

Remoteness seems to inspire profound thinking. The subject matter is relatively narrow as philosophy goes. There is little ethics or metaphysics, and (thankfully) no logical proofs. The Big Picture is the main theme: the meaning of existence and so forth. Nature, of course, plays a major role in these ruminations. It is catalyst and subject, purpose and explanation. My friend the philosopher would probably not be too impressed with the rigor or quality of some of the arguments, but he could not doubt their sincerity.

Keeping Things Whole

In a field
I am the absence
of field.
This is
always the case.

Wherever I am
I am what is missing.

When I walk
I part the air
and always
the air moves in
to fill the spaces
where my body's been.

We all have reasons
for moving.
I move
to keep things whole.

I thought of this poem [by Mark Strand] *while climbing Pharaoh Mountain. I think seeing life at a lake with no one else around, you notice that things are bigger than you in more than one sense. Things are whole.*
—PHARAOH

I would guess that most people who are in the woods for more than a few hours (especially if alone) devote a portion of their time to pondering the meaning of existence. If spending time in the natural world causes us to ponder the meaning of existence, it also helps many better understand their own nature.

This is the final stop on our odyssey from Northville to Lake Placid. It will be 12 days when we come off the trail tomorrow. It has been a most significant trip, although little of note has happened. Finishing the NPT is hardly a monumental feat in the grand scheme of things, but it was an individual challenge of body and will power.
We began the trip with five and lost two because of physical problems and one to lack of will. My feet and knees

held out so I carried on, but not without questioning why I was continuing. The challenge of meeting a goal I had set for myself was a main reason—was I able to finish what I'd begun? This was a key motivational factor, but another soon became apparent—the solitude and remoteness from the world.

This retreat into the wilderness cleared my mind of the usual clutter that fills it. I was removed from my world and found myself with time just to sort through what was important in my life. The trance of plodding along with 60 pounds on your back with only worries being blisters, sore knees, bugs and rain. This gives you hours to just distill what is important. The hours on the trail are followed by the quiet times in camp—sitting by a stream, gazing into the fire, or into the solid ebony of the night sky.

Thoreau in Walden wrote "I went to the woods to live deliberately" and he has hit the point directly. In the woods, thoughts are distilled and all extraneous ones are purged and all that remains is the true essence of life. I came on this hike for a challenge ... but the cleansing of my thoughts and mind has given me a new outlook with which to return to my real world and shown me why I engage in this agony that is called backpacking.

—WANIKA FALLS

The entry above quoted Thoreau, a not infrequent occurrence in the registers. Based on number of entries, he is still the pre-eminent philosopher with the hiking set. However, Henry David isn't the only philosopher hikers quote; the registers are littered with favorite citations, often

THIS AREA IS REALLY MAGIC! THOSE MOUNTAINS, THE BEAUTIFUL LAKE COLDEN, with the notation that they have been left as a gift for others to spur meditation or contemplative thought. This gift, more meaningful than booze or dope (but not as valuable as dry firewood), is reflective of the values hikers bring to the woods.

Whether or not they bring a copy of *Walden*, many people come to the woods seeking enlightenment. I sure have, many times. Sometimes we find it.

Shhhh! Do you hear it?
Pay attention, listen and you
Just might hear the old mother
Speaking to you.
The earth has a voice.
Take a moment to hear her.
And please listen to what she
Has to tell you.
You will be better for it.

—COPPERAS POND

I am on a backpacking trip with Camp Gorham. Yesterday we climbed Giant Mountain, and nothing could ever prepare me for what I felt at the top. I sat some distance from the group with bare feet and legs. The wind cleansed my ears of voices. My fear of heights fell away and I watched the entire world spread out before me. The wind held a chill but I could feel the power behind it warming me.

What finally brought me back to earth was a tiny black ant crawling across my bare feet. As I looked at it closely, I saw nothing more than an ant, but on top of that rock high above everything the ant was more significant than I, with the world at my feet.
–BOQUET RIVER

I sit here in the sun with the constant sound of the water crashing against the rocks. I arrived here yesterday alone, but I am now in the company of at least 30 butterflies who have blessed me with their presence all morning long. How beautiful! I stand among them as one of their own. Unbothered by my presence, they keep gathering. Feeling the soft kisses of their wings I sit here and smile. I think they like me.
—ROCKY FALLS

Of course, there are also those who are merely confused.

We came to find ourselves. If we get back before our return, someone please tell us to go!
—WILCOX LAKE

We conclude this chapter with a quote from Everett Ruess, the artist and writer who wandered the Southwest searching for beauty and adventure before disappearing forever in the Utah wilderness at the age of 20. In many ways Ruess reminds me of Chris McCandless, the wanderer and nature lover who in 1991 was found either starved or accidentally poisoned to death deep in the Alaska bush where he had spent the summer. Some thought McCandless was an inexperienced fool who had no idea what he was getting into. I think he was exactly where he wanted to be.

As to when I shall visit civilization, it will not be soon, I think. I have not tired of the wilderness; rather I enjoy its bounty and the vagrant life I lead, more keenly all the time. I prefer the saddle to the streetcar and star sprinkled sky to a roof, the obscure and difficult trail, leading into the unknown, to any paved highway, and the deep peace of the wild to the discontent bred by cities. Do you blame me then for staying here, where I feel that I belong and am one with the world around me? It is true that I miss intelligent companionship, but there are so few with whom I can share the things that mean so much to me that I have learned to contain myself. It is enough that I am surrounded by beauty. Ruess's last letter [to Everett's brother Waldo], *Nov. 11, 1934.*
—BIG SHALLOW

24

No Place I'd Rather Be

Stopped one night, fishing slow, rain a-plenty, cold, miserable, deer ticks, bears, owls and loons kept us up all night. All in all a miserable experience. Do not recommend to anyone with a sound mind. We had a great time.
—*FISH POND 1*

I must say that finding this notebook was a pleasant surprise. I have enjoyed reading the notes etc. from the unknown fellas who were as blessed as I am. I am solo on a cool, calm and beautiful night. The rivers voice is soothing and refreshing.

This is my first solo backpack & I am loving it … Life right now is truly fantastic and I hope you are well whoever reads this. Good people and wilderness are good things to be in touch with. Thank you for such a wonderful spot to myself. Tomorrow—Dix. Tonight I had an awesome sunset—it put an orange into the whole landscape. Very fulfilling. I will enjoy the fire and then retire. The river is so sweet. Pass on the good news. Peace and have a great trip.
—*BOQUET RIVER*

I F YOU'VE COME THIS FAR, I don't have much else to tell you. Sit back, imagine yourself sitting on the edge of a lean-to, feet dangling above the packed earth, a musical rain falling, and read about others who are happy to be here too.

The beauty and grace of this place warms my hungry soul. Away from civilization I once again become cleansed. My mind rinses itself among the rivers and strong trees. A gentle wind brings along with fresh air, a flavor, so sweet and breathtaking I suck in every molecule I can. A distant bird call reminds me of the fragility of this perfect world, of this brave and unpredictable world. It all carries a scent, the same flavor. I never want to leave.
—COLD RIVER 2

I'm really having the time of my life hear. Like an Indian Summer there is a peaceful breeze with sunlight flowing through the sweet essence of pine trees. I'm calm and comfortably, timelessly numb all over—the best drug in the world—Mother Nature! Thank you Lorne for bringing me here to Wanakena—this has changed my life!
—INLET FLOW

Arrived in high peak region Sunday 18th full of stress from work, wife and an overactive, super imaginative mind. The purity of trailside stream, the crispness of star filled evening sky and the splendor of warm sun filled afternoons with two long term calmed friends have effectively cleansed my mind and focused my thoughts. I now feel directed toward achieving short term and long term goals with renewed vigor and success. I have used many superlatives on this trip and am thankful for that.
—ROCKY FALLS

Just passing through on my return from a "special spot." Gifts were received and given from and to the Creator. The Peace I think comes from being here. I know it is an inspired reflection of what rests within.
—PANTHER POND

Some are especially good at evoking the feel of the place.

A typical unrelenting Adirondack day—a heavy mist, breeze and cold all the way up Dix. After a night of rain the path was muddy, slippery with drenching underbrush. The view at the top was 50 feet maximum with strong gusts and a very heavy mist (rain). So why give up the comforts of the Boquet River Lean To for a cold misery laden trip to Dix? It's the "Adirondack Experience" and can still be appreciated—bright red floral berries, bunchberries and iridescent blue berries and spruces with moisture clinging to every needle, bright green ferns, mosses. The smell of the wet forest—it's all part of the Adirondacks and very much part of the character of the area. This area is so green and lush because of the kind of day we had today so why not live it. We did and it wasn't wonderful, but it was real, and it was the Adirondack experience (drum roll).
—BOQUET RIVER

It's cold. Not freezing, just cold. Very windy—can't hear the brook at all. Of course, maybe because it's frozen... I wish I could stay here forever—one of my favorite places in the world. The sky is wintry—sort of deep blue gray—I heard it's supposed to rain later, and tomorrow—so I'm leaving tonight after some hearty pea soup, crackers, and mocha... Why can't the world be as peaceful and safe as these woods? I wish I could take it with me.
—KLONDIKE

Some never want to leave.

When Bill (my boyfriend) and I hiked here to lean-to #5 some two days ago to find a book full of humorous stories of piranha-like sunfish and the lost sandal, I began to ponder what I should leave for the next hiker to read.

I thought about poetry—too lame or a listing of the sunfish we did catch and the lake trout that got away. Needless to say each time I thought about it I thought about the few

*things that campers in desolate areas enjoy—what "we"—
you the reader, and I the writer have in common.*

*What do we seek when we hike five miles into the
wilderness—tranquility? Solitude? Some of us enjoy the
peacefulness away from our nagging, annoying significant
other. Some seek time to spend with one another. Some
fathers bring their daughters and son to fulfill the "bonding" that disappear with school and work. The elderly
might seek their youthful memories of carving initials into
the tree trunks and running naked through the sweet summer air.*

*Is it something in the air of a smoke filled campsite? Or
the loons, which sing their hallow-filled notes in the stillness of the morning? The chipmunk who climbs upon my
shoulder and bite my toes because he thinks its food? I seek
the stillness.*

*I enjoy bathing naked in the morning sun and fly fish-
ing in the painted evening dusk. I enjoy watching a man
building a fire, as he would build his life—one log at a
time. I enjoy the chill of the night air bringing a rosy hue
to my cheeks and the warmth of a touch of another hand.
I enjoy a stiff heel and a dirty earth. I enjoy the birds, and
the echo of a child's laugh across the lake. But most of all I
enjoy the company of myself, mother earth and the man
that I love, and tomorrow I will enjoy the walk home.*
—STONY POND

Two final entries, which followed one another in the Duck
Hole register. The first author identified herself as a college
sophomore.

*People tell me regularly that it all gets to be the same
after a while: the woods, the lakes, the mountains. I
give them a baffled look of incomprehension. Every time
I go out I find something new, something wonderful.
Every sunset and sunrise is just as magnificent as my first.*

I never tire of hearing a loon or of looking at the trees. They really are all different and individual, just like people.

My friends tell me that I'm overly sentimental, and maybe I am, but to me the Adirondacks are more than just woods, lakes and mountains. They are my home. For generations my family has been here and will continue to flourish in the magic of these mountains.

Last afternoon while finding the rhythm of my pace the familiar thoughts came to mind: beauty of the country, fascination with the wild, why did I bring so much stuff? Will my feet blister, when are we going to get there?!!

But now that we've arrived and have had a good rest and swim, I'm just soaking in the relaxing atmosphere and appreciating the wonderful system you've built here—lean-tos, registers and such. But mostly I'm consumed with the overwhelming desire to take the young woman on the previous page as my wife.

Amen.

Leave No Trace

ADK supports the seven principles of the Leave No Trace program:

1. Plan Ahead and Prepare
   - Know the regulations and special considerations for the area you'll visit.
   - Prepare for extreme weather, hazards, and emergencies.
   - Travel in groups of less than ten people to minimize impacts.

2. Travel and Camp on Durable Surfaces
   - Hike in the middle of the trail; stay off of vegetation.
   - Camp in designated sites where possible.
   - In other areas, don't camp within 150 feet of water or a trail.

3. Dispose of Waste Properly
   - Pack out all trash (including toilet paper), leftover food, and litter.
   - Use existing privies, or dig a cat hole five to six inches deep, then cover hole.
   - Wash yourself and dishes at least 150 feet from water.

4. Leave What You Find
   - Leave rocks, plants, and other natural objects as you find them.
   - Let photos, drawings, or journals help to capture your memories.
   - Do not build structures or furniture or dig trenches.

5. Minimize Campfire Impacts
   - Use a portable stove to avoid the lasting impact of a campfire.
   - Where fires are permitted, use existing fire rings and only collect downed wood.
   - Burn all fires to ash, put out campfires completely, then hide traces of fire.

6. Respect Wildlife
   - Observe wildlife from a distance.
   - Avoid wildlife during mating, nesting, and other sensitive times.
   - Control pets at all times, and clean up after them.

7. Be Considerate of Other Visitors
   - Respect other visitors and protect the quality of their experience.
   - Let natural sounds prevail; avoid loud sounds and voices.
   - Be courteous and yield to other users on the trail.

For further information on Leave No Trace principles, log on to www.lnt.org.

General Forest Preserve Camping Regulations

THE REGULATIONS regarding tenting and the use of shelters in the Adirondack and Catskill parks are relatively unrestrictive when compared to those found in other popular backpacking areas in this country and Canada. Current regulations should be seen as the minimum standard campers must meet to responsibly use the public lands that comprise the Forest Preserve.

Complete regulations are available from the DEC by calling, writing, or consulting their Web site at www.dec.state.ny.us/website/dlf/publands/bacrule.html. In addition, they are posted at major trail access points.

The following are the most important regulations all campers must obey when camping in the Forest Preserve. Note that special restrictions apply in the High Peaks region, specifically the Eastern and Western zones of the High Peaks Wilderness and in the Dix Mountain and Giant Mountain wilderness areas. (See ADK's *Adirondack Trails: High Peaks Region*, p. 25.)

GROUP SIZE

1. Camping groups are limited to nine throughout the Forest Preserve.*
2. In the Adirondack Canoe Zone of the High Peaks Wilderness Area and in most other areas of the Park, groups of up to twelve are allowed—but only with a permit from the DEC forest ranger in whose district the trip starts. (One should contact the ranger by mail either directly or through DEC Headquarters in Ray Brook several weeks in advance. Telephone contact is not guaranteed given rangers' unpre-

dictable schedules. Remember that in most cases one is calling a private home when trying to contact a forest ranger by telephone.)

Affiliated groups whose total size exceeds group size limits must maintain a separation distance of at least 1.0 mile (1.6 kilometers) when either camping or day hiking to comply with the above regulations.

CAMPSITES

1. Designated sites marked with an official marker are defined as an area within fifteen feet (five meters) of the marker.
2. Pristine or at-large sites must be located at least 150 feet (46 meters) from roads, trails, or water sources.*
3. No camping is permitted above 4000 feet (1219 meters) at any time of the year.
4. Camping between 3500 and 4000 feet (1067 and 1219 meters) is allowed at designated sites only. Currently Sno-Bird and Lake Arnold, in the High Peaks, are the only designated sites found between these elevations.

LEAN-TOS

1. Must be shared by groups up to the capacity (eight persons) of the shelter.
2. No plastic may be used to close off the front of the shelter.
3. No nails or other permanent fastener may be used to affix a tarp. Rope, however, may be used to tie a nylon or canvas tarp to a lean-to.
4. No tent may be pitched inside a lean-to.
5. No tent may be pitched next to a lean-to to increase capacity.

---

* Special regulations apply in parts of the High Peaks region. See ADK's *Adirondack Trails: High Peaks Region*, ADK's Web site, or DEC's Web site.

BEAR CANISTERS

Bears in many parts of the High Peaks have figured out the long-popular campers' technique of hanging food from a rope strung between two trees. Thus the DEC is now strongly encouraging—in some cases requiring—the use of bear-resistant, food-storage canisters.

These can be obtained from many outdoor retailers, borrowed from many ADK chapters, or rented or purchased from the High Peaks Information Center at ADK's Heart Lake Program Center. The canisters also protect food from many smaller forest creatures.

The DEC's current management goal with respect to bears is to educate campers about proper food storage. Bears unable to get food from campers will, it is hoped, return to their natural diet. Thus campers play an important role in helping to restore the natural balance between bears and humans. Losing one's food to a bear should be recognized as a critical failure in achieving this goal.

CAMPFIRES

1. Campfires are allowed at designated campsites and legal at-large sites only.* Only dead and down wood may be used for fires.
2. Build fires only on nonflammable surfaces such as rock, sand, or mineral soil. The organic matter and soil typical of Adirondack forests is highly flammable and will burn long after the campfire is supposedly out. (A major fire on Noonmark Mt. started this way in 1999.)

OTHER REGULATIONS

1. Do not use soap or detergent in any water source.

2. Do not dispose of food scraps in any water source. (Compliance with numbers 1 and 2 requires that all dish washing or bathing be done at least 150 feet from any water source.)

3. Glass containers are prohibited.

4. Quiet must be observed from 10 PM to 7 AM.

5. Audio devices must not be audible outside the immediate campsite.

6. All trash must be packed out.

7. All human waste must be disposed of properly. Use privies where available; otherwise bury waste six to eight inches below the surface and 150 feet from any trail or water source.

8. Do not feed any animals.

9. Store food properly to keep it away from animals—particularly bears.*

---

* Special regulations apply in parts of the High Peaks region. See ADK's *Adirondack Trails: High Peaks Region*, ADK's Web site, or DEC's Web site.

Acknowledgments

FIRST AND FOREMOST, thanks to all those who have adopted and cared for lean-tos past, present, and future. Adopters donate their time and energy to ensure that lean-tos are available to provide shelter from the elements to the sick and weary. There's no telling how many lives have been saved as a result of their efforts. Everybody who spends time in a lean-to owes them a big thank you. Thanks are also due to the State of New York and, more specifically, the forest rangers who patrol the woods. Rangers also routinely assist with lean-to maintenance and are helpful and cooperative partners in the lean-to adoption program.

Thanks also to the Adirondack Mountain Club for making the approximately 150 registers in its collection available to me and for supporting this book. I hope it will have been worth the Club's time and money. Several individual adopters and rangers gave me access to registers in their care, for which I am very appreciative.

Maggie Phillips, then in junior high school, typed up most of the entries from which I chose the material for this book. Because I collected perhaps five times as many entries as are found here, it was quite a task. Her mother, Michele Phillips, facilitated her doing so. Thanks to them both.

Ann Hough designed the text, created the layout, and mined the registers for additional images. All credit to her for the text's visual appeal. Nicole Farrell reviewed numerous proofs and handled an array of production concerns. I really appreciate her work inasmuch as I never heard a word about most of them. Thanks to Tamara Dever, who designed the cover on extremely short notice.

Tom Wheeler, Jim Schneider, John Schneider, Chris Jerome, and Neal Burdick read a late draft of the manuscript and offered excellent suggestions and advice, some of which I followed. Thanks to them all, especially Neal for helping to solve the vexing subtitle problem.

Biggest thanks of all go to my editor, Andrea Masters, who was unfailingly supportive in my efforts to write this book. Andrea provided good advice, steered me in the right direction when I was floundering, and, when a kick in the pants was needed, she supplied it in the gentlest possible way. This book wouldn't have happened without her help. Thanks are also due to past ADK Publications Director John Kettlewell, who also provided advice and encouragement, made the Club's resources available to me, and helped with the publication process.

Finally, on a personal note, thanks are due to my father, who took me into the woods at an early age and fostered my love of the outdoors, as well as to the various hiking companions who have accompanied me over the years. You have all been great friends and have enriched my life. This book wouldn't have been possible without you. I look forward to our next hike.

About the Author

STUART MESINGER lives in South Glens Falls, New York, with his wife Peg and his son Will. A native of Virginia, he attended college in the foothills of St. Lawrence County, where he fell in love with the Adirondacks. He works as a planning consultant to pay the bills, but his first love is the outdoors. He is an avid hiker, paddler, and fisherman. If this book is any kind of success at all, he plans to write another one.

Adirondack Mountain Club

INFORMATION CENTERS

The ADK Member Services Center in Lake George and the ADK Heart Lake Program Center near Lake Placid, at the head of the Van Hoevenberg Trail, offer ADK publications and other merchandise for sale, as well as backcountry and general Adirondack information, educational displays, outdoor equipment, and snacks.

LODGES AND CAMPGROUND

Adirondak Loj, on the shores of Heart Lake, offers year-round accommodations in private and family rooms, a coed bunkroom, and cabins. It is accessible by car, and ample trailhead parking is available.

The Adirondak Loj Wilderness Campground, located on the Heart Lake property, offers thirty-four campsites, sixteen Adirondack-style lean-tos, and three tent cabins.

Johns Brook Lodge (JBL), located near Keene Valley, is a seasonal backcountry facility located in prime hiking country. It is 3.5 mi from the nearest road and is accessible only on foot. Facilities include coed bunkrooms or small family rooms. Cabins near JBL are available year-round.

Both lodges offer home-cooked meals and trail lunches.

JOIN US

We are a nonprofit membership organization that brings together people with interests in recreation, conservation, and environmental education in the New York State Forest Preserve.

ADKers choose from friendly outings, for those just getting started with local chapters, to Adirondack backpacks and international treks. Learn gradually through chapter outings or attend one of our schools, workshops, or other programs.

Membership Benefits

• Discovery: ADK can broaden your horizons by introducing you to new places, people, recreational activities, and interests.

• *Adirondac* Magazine

• Member Discounts: 20% off on guidebooks, maps, and other ADK publications; discount on lodge stays; discount on educational programs

• Satisfaction: Know that you're doing your part so future generations can enjoy the wilderness as you do.

• Chapter Participation: Experience the fun of outings and other social activities and the reward of working on trails, conservation, and education projects at the local level. You can also join as a member at large.

• Volunteer Opportunities: Give something back. There are many rewarding options in trail work, conservation and advocacy, and educational projects.

For more information

ADK Member Services Center
(Exit 21 off the Northway, I-87)
814 Goggins Road, Lake George, NY 12845-4117

ADK Heart Lake Program Center
P.O. Box 867, Lake Placid, NY 12946-0867

ADK Public Affairs Office
301 Hamilton Street, Albany, NY 12210-1738

Information: 518-668-4447
Membership: 800-395-8080
Publications and merchandise: 800-395-8080
Education: 518-523-3441
Facilities' reservations: 518-523-3441
Public affairs: 518-449-3870
E-mail: adkinfo@adk.org
Web site: www.adk.org

ADK Publications

FOREST PRESERVE SERIES

Adirondack Trails: High Peaks Region (Vol. 1)
Adirondack Trails: Northern Region (Vol. 2)
Adirondack Trails: Central Region (Vol. 3)
Adirondack Trails: Northville–Placid Trail (Vol. 4)
Adirondack Trails: West-Central Region (Vol. 5)
Adirondack Trails: Eastern Region (Vol. 6)
Adirondack Trails: Southern Region (Vol. 7)
Catskill Trails (Vol. 8)

BOOKS

Adirondack Canoe Waters: North Flow
Adirondack Mountain Club Canoe and Kayak Guide to East-Central New York State
Adirondack Mountain Club Canoe Guide to Western & Central New York State
An Adirondack Passage: The Cruise of the Canoe *Sairy Gamp*
An Adirondack Sampler I: Day Hikes for All Seasons
Catskill Day Hikes for All Seasons
Climbing in the Adirondacks: A Guide to Rock & Ice Routes
Forests & Trees of the Adirondack High Peaks Region
Kids on the Trail! Hiking with Children in the Adirondacks
Ski and Snowshoe Trails in the Adirondacks
The Adirondack Reader
Views from on High: Fire Tower Trails in the Adirondacks and Catskills
Winterwise: A Backpacker's Guide

MAPS

Trails of the Adirondack High Peaks Region
Trails of the Adirondack Northern Region
Trails of the Adirondack Central Region
Northville–Placid Trail
Trails of the Adirondack West-Central Region
Trails of the Adirondack Eastern Region
Trails of the Adirondack Southern Region
National Geographic Trails Illustrated Maps of the Adirondacks

Adirondack Mountain Club, Inc.

To order:
800-395-8080
(Mon.–Sat., 8:30–5:00)
24/7: **www.adk.org**

ADIRONDACK MOUNTAIN CLUB CALENDAR
Price list available upon request